Virginia SOL Coach,
New Gold Edition, English,
Grade 3

triumphlearning™

Virginia SOL Coach, New Gold Edition, English, Grade 3
207VA
ISBN-13: 978-0-7836-8139-9

Cover Image: The cardinal is the state bird of Virginia. © Elizabeth Rosen/Morgan Gaynin, Inc.

Triumph Learning® 136 Madison Avenue, 7th Floor, New York, NY 10016

© 2012 Triumph Learning, LLC
Coach is an imprint of Triumph Learning®

Printed in the United States of America.

10 9 8 7 6 5 4 3 2

DEAR STUDENT,

Welcome to *Coach*—your learning path to success!

This book provides **instruction** and **practice** that will help you master the skills you need to know. It also gives you practice answering the kinds of questions you will see on your **state test**.

The *Coach* book is organized into **chapters** and **lessons**. Each lesson explains a topic that's important in your **study** of English Language Arts.

Each of the **lessons** has three parts. The first part walks you through the **skill** so you know what it is. The second part gives you an **example**, with hints to help your thinking about the skill. The third part of the lesson gives you practice with the skill to see how well you **understand** it. You can check your understanding of each topic by answering the questions at the end of the lesson and in the **chapter reviews**.

We wish you lots of **success** this year, and are glad *Coach* can be a part of it!

Sincerely,

THE COACH TEAM

Table of Contents

Student Letter 3
English Standards of Learning Correlation Chart 6

			Standards of Learning
Chapter 1	**Vocabulary** 9		
Lesson 1	Vowel Patterns 10		3.3.a
Lesson 2	Multisyllabic Words 16		3.3.b
● Lesson 3	Roots and Affixes 22		3.4.b
Lesson 4	Synonyms, Antonyms, and Homophones 28		3.4.a, 3.4.b
Lesson 5	Meaning Clues, Structure Clues, and Phonetics 34		3.4.c
Lesson 6	Context Clues 40		3.4.d
Lesson 7	Content Area Vocabulary 46		3.4.e, 3.4.f
Lesson 8	Using a Dictionary, Thesaurus, and Glossary 52		3.4.g
Chapter 1 Review 58			

Chapter 2	**Reading Comprehension** 65		
● Lesson 9	Fiction and Nonfiction 66		3.5.a, 3.5.e, 3.5.i, 3.6.a, 3.6.k
● Lesson 10	Ask and Answer Questions 72		3.5.f, 3.6.d
● Lesson 11	Main Idea and Supporting Details 78		3.5.i–k, 3.6.f–h, 3.6.j
Lesson 12	Compare and Contrast 84		3.5.d, 3.6.i
Lesson 13	Problem and Solution 92		3.5.h
Lesson 14	Predictions 98		3.5.c
Lesson 15	Make Inferences and Draw Conclusions 104		3.5.b, 3.5.g, 3.6.b, 3.6.e
● Lesson 16	Text Features 110		3.6.c, 3.7.b
Chapter 2 Review 116			

Chapter 3 Writing . . . . 123 **Standards of Learning**

Lesson 17 Author's Purpose and Audience 124 3.9.a

Lesson 18 Prewriting Strategies 130 3.9.b, 3.9.e

Lesson 19 Topic Sentences and Paragraphs 136 3.9.c, 3.9.d, 3.9.f

Lesson 20 Revising Writing 142 3.9.g

Lesson 21 Writing a Short Report 148 3.7.a, 3.11.a–d, 3.12

Chapter 3 Review 154

Chapter 4 Editing and Grammar 159

Lesson 22 Spelling 160 3.10.j

Lesson 23 Articles and Abbreviations 166 3.10.g, 3.10.i

Lesson 24 Possessives and Contractions 172 3.10.e, 3.10.h

Lesson 25 Verb Tenses 178 3.10.d

Lesson 26 Sentence Structure 184 3.10.a–c, 3.10.f

Chapter 4 Review 190

Glossary 196

Mechanics Toolbox 203

Grade Three

Reading continues to be a priority in third grade. Emphasis is on learning about words, reading text with fluency and expression, and learning comprehension strategies. The student will read a variety of fiction and nonfiction texts, which relate to all areas of the curriculum. The student will use effective communication skills in group activities and will present brief oral reports. Reading comprehension strategies will be applied in all subjects, with emphasis on materials that reflect the Standards of Learning in mathematics, science, and history and social science. The student will plan, draft, revise, and edit stories, simple explanations, and short reports. In addition, the student will gather and use information from print and electronic sources. The student also will write legibly in cursive.

Reading

3.3   The student will apply word-analysis skills when reading.
- a) Use knowledge of regular and irregular vowel patterns. **(Lesson 1)**
- b) Decode regular multisyllabic words. **(Lesson 2)**

3.4   The student will expand vocabulary when reading.
- a) Use knowledge of homophones. **(Lesson 4)**
- b) Use knowledge of roots, affixes, synonyms, and antonyms. **(Lessons 3, 4)**
- c) Apply meaning clues, language structure, and phonetic strategies. **(Lesson 5)**
- d) Use context to clarify meaning of unfamiliar words. **(Lesson 6)**
- e) Discuss meanings of words and develop vocabulary by listening and reading a variety of texts. **(Lessons 6–8)**
- f) Use vocabulary from other content areas. **(Lesson 7)**
- g) Use word reference resources including the glossary, dictionary, and thesaurus. **(Lesson 8)**

3.5   The student will read and demonstrate comprehension of fictional text and poetry.
- a) Set a purpose for reading. **(Lesson 9)**
- b) Make connections between previous experiences and reading selections. **(Lesson 15)**
- c) Make, confirm, or revise predictions. **(Lesson 14)**
- d) Compare and contrast settings, characters, and events. **(Lesson 12)**
- e) Identify the author's purpose. **(Lesson 17)**
- f) Ask and answer questions about what is read. **(Lesson 10)**
- g) Draw conclusions about text. **(Lesson 15)**
- h) Identify the problem and solution. **(Lesson 13)**
- i) Identify the main idea. **(Lesson 11)**
- j) Identify supporting details. **(Lesson 11)**
- k) Use reading strategies to monitor comprehension throughout the reading process. **(Lessons 10–16)**
- l) Differentiate between fiction and nonfiction. **(Lesson 9)**
- m) Read with fluency and accuracy.

3.6   The student will continue to read and demonstrate comprehension of nonfiction texts.
   a) Identify the author's purpose. **(Lesson 17)**
   b) Use prior and background knowledge as context for new learning. **(Lesson 15)**
   c) Preview and use text features. **(Lesson 16)**
   d) Ask and answer questions about what is read. **(Lesson 10)**
   e) Draw conclusions based on text. **(Lesson 15)**
   f) Summarize major points found in nonfiction texts. **(Lesson 11)**
   g) Identify the main idea. **(Lesson 11)**
   h) Identify supporting details. **(Lesson 11)**
   i) Compare and contrast the characteristics of biographies and autobiographies. **(Lessons 9, 12)**
   j) Use reading strategies to monitor comprehension throughout the reading process. **(Lessons 10–16)**
   k) Identify new information gained from reading. **(Lesson 16)**
   l) Read with fluency and accuracy.

3.7   The student will demonstrate comprehension of information from a variety of print and electronic resources.
   a) Use encyclopedias and other reference books, including online reference materials. **(Lesson 21)**
   b) Use table of contents, indices, and charts. **(Lesson 16)**

Writing

3.9   The student will write for a variety of purposes.
   a) Identify the intended audience. **(Lesson 17)**
   b) Use a variety of prewriting strategies. **(Lesson 18)**
   c) Write a clear topic sentence focusing on the main idea. **(Lesson 19)**
   d) Write a paragraph on the same topic. **(Lesson 19)**
   e) Use strategies for organization of information and elaboration according to the type of writing. **(Lesson 20)**
   f) Include details that elaborate the main idea. **(Lesson 20)**
   g) Revise writing for clarity of content using specific vocabulary and information. **(Lesson 20)**

3.10   The student will edit writing for correct grammar, capitalization, punctuation, and spelling.
        a) Use complete sentences. **(Lesson 26)**
        b) Use transition words to vary sentence structure. **(Lesson 19)**
        c) Use the word *I* in compound subjects. **(Lesson 26)**
        d) Use past and present verb tense. **(Lesson 25)**
        e) Use singular possessives. **(Lesson 24)**
        f) Use commas in a simple series. **(Lesson 26)**
        g) Use simple abbreviations. **(Lesson 23)**
        h) Use apostrophes in contractions with pronouns and in possessives. **(Lesson 24)**
        i) Use the articles *a*, *an*, and *the* correctly. **(Lesson 23)**
        j) Use correct spelling for frequently used sight words, including irregular plurals. **(Lesson 22)**

3.11   The student will write a short report.
        a) Construct questions about the topic. **(Lesson 21)**
        b) Identify appropriate resources. **(Lesson 21)**
        c) Collect and organize information about the topic into a short report. **(Lesson 21)**
        d) Understand the difference between plagiarism and using own words. **(Lesson 21)**

3.12   The student will use available technology for reading and writing. **(Lesson 21)**

CHAPTER

Vocabulary

Lesson 1 Vowel Patterns
3.3.a

Lesson 2 Multisyllabic Words
3.3.b

Lesson 3 Roots and Affixes
3.4.b

Lesson 4 Synonyms, Antonyms, and Homophones
3.4.a, 3.4.b

Lesson 5 Meaning Clues, Structure Clues, and Phonetics
3.4.c

Lesson 6 Context Clues
3.4.d

Lesson 7 Content Area Vocabulary
3.4.e, 3.4.f

Lesson 8 Using a Dictionary, Thesaurus, and Glossary
3.4.g

Chapter 1 Review

1 Vowel Patterns

3.3.a

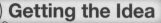 Getting the Idea

Each word in the English language has a vowel in it. The English **vowels** are a, e, i, o, and u. The way the letters join in a word changes how the word sounds. When a vowel comes between two consonants, it has a short vowel sound. Listen to the short vowel sounds in *bat*, *pet*, *pig*, *hot*, and *gum*. Here are some other words that have short vowel sounds.

Short Vowel Sounds

a	apple, clam, alphabet, flash, hamster
e	fell, mess, nectar, bend, exam
i	in, limit, thrill, lizard, litter
o	volcano, clock, robin, observe, otter
u	rusty, trust, number, dust, thumb

Say the letter a aloud. This is what the long a sounds like. Long vowel sounds can be formed by adding a silent e to the end of a word. For example, the silent e changes the word *cap* to *cape*. Here are some words with long vowel sounds.

Long Vowel Sounds

a	graceful, cake, whale, label, wave
e	Egypt, evening, equal, freeze, week
i	glide, write, dinosaur, idea, ice, island
o	nose, robot, bone, ocean, open
u	uniform, music, cube, tune, huge

Sometimes the letter *r* controls the sound of the vowel that comes before it. The short *a* in *cat* has a different sound from the short *a* in *car* because the *r* changes the sound of the *a*. Look at the words below.

a	car, part, shark, start, arm
e	river, water, flower, paper, later
i	dirt, shirt, bird, girl, chirp
o	storm, horse, fork, worn, north
u	turn, hurt, surf, fur, blur

When you see a double *o* in words (oo), there are two possible sounds the letters can make. Here are some examples.

double o	book, look, wool, hood, stood, good
long u sound (oo)	pool, school, moon, soon, goose, tooth

When two vowels appear together in a word, they often make the long vowel sound of the first vowel. Here are some examples.

ai	rain, paid, gain, raise, chain, train
ea	leap, leaf, read, mean, meat, peanut
oa	boat, float, roam, coach, goal, load

Thinking It Through

Read the following paragraph, and then answer the question that follows.

Monica's favorite game is "Heroes Now." There are three ways to win the game. One way is to beat the other player in a battle. The second way is to be the first to get through a <u>maze</u>. The third is to be the one who finds the magic ring hidden in the game. Monica was ready to win. The problem was, she just didn't know how she would do it!

What kind of vowel sound is used in the underlined word in the paragraph? Tell how you know.

_____

_____

_____

_____

_____

HINT   Think about whether the vowel sound is short or long. Look at how the word is spelled.

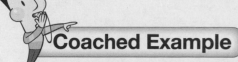

Coached Example

Read the passage and answer the questions.

When people think of an artist, they may think of someone who has skill in drawing. But artists do more than just draw or <u>paint</u>. They see the world in a new and creative way. An artist does not even have to draw or use paints at all. Some artists work with clay. Others use objects that they find, such as seashells, to make collages, a special kind of art. Photographs, films, and videos are also kinds of art. So when you see a beautiful painting in a museum, think about what it means to make a work of art.

---

1. Which word has the same vowel sound as <u>paint</u>?

    A. piece

    B. iceberg

    C. train

    D. small

    HINT The word *paint* has a long vowel sound. What long vowel sound does it make?

2. Which of the following words from the passage has a short *i* sound?

    A. artists

    B. photographs

    C. kinds

    D. special

    HINT Review the chart in the lesson to understand the vowel sound the short *i* makes.

Lesson Practice

Use the Reading Guide to help you understand the passage.

Reading Guide

What kind of vowel pattern is used in the word *looked*?

Which *i* in *inside* makes the long vowel sound?

Which vowel sound is used in the word *puzzle*?

Think of a word that has the same vowel sound as *gold*.

The Rainy Day

Jessica <u>looked</u> out the window with disappointment. She had not expected it to be pouring outside. All of her plans were for outdoor activities. She had wanted to jog in the park, rake the leaves, and then go to the community swimming <u>pool</u>. Now she was <u>stuck</u> <u>inside</u> all day.

She looked up the weather report on her computer and sighed. It would be <u>raining</u> for the next three days. Then she took out the <u>puzzle</u> her mother had given her for her birthday last year. At first, she wasn't sure she wanted to do it. But she knew she had to pass the time on this rainy day. So she ripped open the box and soon sat down at the kitchen table.

Within half an hour Jessica had turned over all the puzzle pieces so that they faced up. Then she separated the edges from the middle pieces. She had forgotten how much fun she used to have making puzzles when she was younger. This looked like a challenge, but she was ready for it! She was starting to put the pieces together a little at a time. She could see the pattern of blue and <u>gold</u> coming to life on the table. Thank goodness for rainy days!

Answer the following questions.

1. Which word from the passage has the same vowel sound as <u>stuck</u>?

   A. outside

   B. rainy

   C. puzzle

   D. ripped

2. Which word from the passage has a vowel sound that is changed by the letter *r*?

   A. mother

   B. rainy

   C. ready

   D. ripped

3. Which word from the passage has the long *o* sound?

   A. pouring

   B. jog

   C. open

   D. younger

4. Which word from the passage makes the same *oo* sound as <u>pool</u>?

   A. looked

   B. soon

   C. outdoor

   D. gold

5. Say the word <u>raining</u> from the passage. Why do the vowels *ai* in the word have the long *a* sound?

   _____

   _____

   _____

   _____

   _____

2 Multisyllabic Words

3.3.b

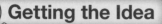 **Getting the Idea**

When you speak, the words you say are divided into syllables. A **syllable** is a small unit of sound. Say the word *forget*. The word is divided into two syllables: *for* and *get*. The list below has words with just one syllable. Most words are separated into parts with just one vowel sound per syllable.

sing	lost	day	green
hand	say	tree	tie
shake	kite	shoe	might

Words with more than one syllable are called **multisyllabic words**. You can count the syllables in a word by clapping for each syllable as you hear it. For example, if you clap as you say each separate part of the word *incredible*, you have clapped four times. The four syllables in the word are: *in • cred • i • ble*.

Another way to find the number of syllables in a word is to count the syllables on your fingers. For example, hold up a finger for each syllable you hear in the word *believe*. You will hold up two fingers. The word has two syllables.

Think about how many syllables are in the word *difficult*. If you count them out, you will find that there are three syllables.

If you are unsure about how to pronounce a word, the dictionary divides words into syllables. There, you may find the words written like this: cre • a • tive. The dictionary shows how the word is divided into different syllable sounds.

Extra word parts that come before or after a word add to the number of syllables. For example, the word *sing* has one syllable, but *singing* has two syllables. The word *tie* has one syllable, but *untie* has two syllables.

When you say a multisyllabic word, one of the syllables is stressed more than the others. For example, in the word *tomato*, you say toe•MAY•toe. You stress the middle syllable. It would not be correct to pronounce the word as toe•may•TOE. A dictionary shows you how to pronounce a word by showing which syllable to stress.

Look at the chart below. For each word, the chart shows the number of syllables. It also shows which syllable to stress. The stressed syllable is in capital letters.

	Number of syllables	Stress
powerfully	4	POW•er•ful•ly
completely	3	com•PLETE•ly
understandable	5	un•der•STAND•a•ble
paragraph	3	PAR•a•graph
naturally	4	NAT•u•ral•ly

Thinking It Through

Read the following paragraph, and then answer the questions that follow.

I looked out my bedroom window. There was a strange object in my backyard. It looked like a spaceship. <u>Suddenly</u>, a door opened. A purple alien stepped out. "I am Og," it said in a loud voice. I yelled for my dad.

How many syllables are in the word <u>suddenly</u>? Which syllable is stressed?

_____

_____

_____

_____

HINT Use a method to count syllables, such as clapping or counting on your fingers. Listen as you say the word aloud to tell which syllable is stressed.

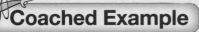

Coached Example

Read the passage and answer the questions.

Denise heard the typing sound of her dad's <u>computer</u> in the other room. She looked at her clock from her bed. It was 3:00 in the afternoon. Denise hated being sick in bed, but she knew it would be difficult for her just to stand up. She let her head fall back onto the pillow and closed her eyes. Her mom would be in soon to give her medicine and check her fever with the thermometer. She was not sure if any of the medicine was helping. But her mom said she would feel even worse if she didn't have it. Oh, how she hated being sick!

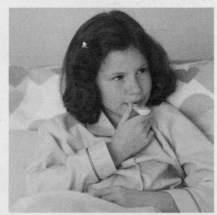

1. How many syllables are in the word <u>computer</u>?

   A. 2

   B. 3

   C. 4

   D. 5

   HINT Count the number of syllables by clapping or counting on your fingers.

2. Which word from the passage has the MOST number of syllables?

   A. computer

   B. afternoon

   C. thermometer

   D. medicine

   HINT Count the number of syllables in each word to compare them.

Lesson Practice

Use the Reading Guide to help you understand the passage.

Reading Guide

How many syllables are in Oliver's name?

What other word in the story has the same number of syllables as *remember*?

Which syllable in *sneakers* is stressed more than the other?

Oliver Goes to the Mall

Oliver and his father went to the mall on Saturday. Oliver needed new clothes for school. The mall was very crowded.

"Remember what to do if you get lost," Dad said. "If you don't see me, go to the man behind the front desk. He wears a uniform. He finds people who are lost. You won't be disappearing from *me* so easily!" He winked at Oliver and they began their shopping.

Oliver and his father bought some T-shirts. They also bought a new book bag. Next, they looked for sneakers. Oliver sat down while his father walked over to the rows of sneakers against the wall. Oliver's father was gone for a long time. Finally, Oliver got tired of waiting, so he got up and walked around. He looked at the variety of shoes. Then, suddenly, he could not see his father any longer. There were so many shoppers that Oliver kept bumping into people.

Then, Oliver remembered what his father had said. So he went to the front desk for help. "My father got lost," Oliver told the guard.

The guard smiled and asked his name. Then the guard said over the loudspeaker: "Will Oliver's father please come to the front desk?"

Soon Oliver's father arrived. Oliver was glad to see him.

Answer the following questions.

1. Which word from the passage has three syllables?

    A. father

    B. uniform

    C. school

    D. crowded

2. Which syllable in the word disappearing is stressed more than the others?

    A. first

    B. second

    C. third

    D. fourth

3. Which word has the same number of syllables as uniform?

    A. father

    B. guard

    C. people

    D. loudspeaker

4. Read this sentence from the passage.

    Then, suddenly, he could not see his father any longer.

    Which word in the sentence has the most syllables?

    A. suddenly

    B. could

    C. father

    D. longer

5. Which words from paragraphs 2 and 3 have four syllables each?

    _____

    _____

    _____

    _____

3 Roots and Affixes

3.4.b

Getting the Idea

If you see a word you do not know while reading, you can look it up in a dictionary. Most dictionaries give you the root of a word. A **root** is the main part of a word. To find the root of a word, look for the shorter word hidden inside it. If you can identify the root in one word, then you can figure out the meaning of another word with the same root. For example, the root *graph* means "write." So, when you see the words *autograph* and *biography*, you know they have something to do with writing. Sometimes a root is a complete word. Then it is called a **root word**.

An **affix** is a group of letters (or word part) that is added to the beginning or end of a root or root word. An affix changes the meaning of the root word, or makes a new word. A **prefix** is a group of letters (or word part) that is added to the beginning of a root or root word. A prefix changes the meaning of a word or makes a new word. Look at this chart of prefixes and their meanings.

Words with Prefixes

Prefix	Meaning	Example	New Meaning
dis-	opposite, not	disobey	not obey
mis-	wrong, wrongly	misspell	spell wrongly
pre-	before	preview	view before
re-	again, back	rebuild	build again
un-	not	unkind	not kind

Adding a prefix to a root word does not usually change the spelling of the root word. Look at the examples below.

- dis- + appear = disappear
- mis- + treat = mistreat
- pre- + write = prewrite
- re- + read = reread
- un- + happy = unhappy

Thinking It Through 1

Read the following sentences. Write them correctly on the lines provided. If the sentence is correct, write "correct as is."

1. Anna was <u>unnable</u> to carry the box.

_____

HINT Remember, adding a prefix to a root word does not usually change the spelling of the root word.

2. The twins always <u>dissagree</u> about everything.

_____

HINT Think about the root word and the prefix in the underlined word

3. We want to <u>return</u> to the museum before it closes.

_____

4. Julie made one <u>misstake</u> on the quiz.

_____

5. Kathy needed to <u>preeheat</u> the oven before baking the cookies.

_____

6. The two puppies looked <u>dissimilar</u>.

_____

A **suffix** is a group of letters (or word part) that is added to the·end of a root or root word. Like a prefix, a suffix changes a word's meaning or makes a new word. To figure out the new word's meaning, join the meaning of the root word with the meaning of the suffix.

Words with Suffixes

Suffix	Meaning	Example	New Meaning
-able, -ible	able	breakable, forcible	able to be broken, able to be forced
-ed	in the past	walked	to walk in the past
-er	more	bigger	more big
-est	most	tallest	the most tall
-ful	full of	hopeful	full of hope
-ish	like	foolish	like a fool
-less	without	careless	without any care
-ly	in a certain way	slowly	in a slow way
-ness	a state or quality	goodness	state of being good
-y	full of, state of being	furry	full of fur

Sometimes the spelling of the root word is not changed when adding a suffix: *care + -ful = careful*. Other·times, the spelling of the root word changes when certain suffixes are added. For example, *happy* becomes *happi* when adding the suffix *-ness*. Also, words ending in silent *e* drop the *e* before adding the suffix *-y: noise + -y = noisy*. Look at the different spellings of some suffixes and root words.

- study + -ed = studied
- fancy + -ful = fanciful
- rely + -able = reliable
- wide + -er = wider
- wide + -ly = widely
- shine + -est = shiniest

- shop + -ing = shopping
- ship + -ment = shipment
- chew + -y = chewy
- scare + -y = scary
- style + -ish = stylish
- fear + -less = fearless

Thinking It Through 2

Read the following sentences. Write them correctly on the lines provided. If the sentence is correct, write "correct as is."

1. Lena made <u>carless</u> mistakes on the test.

_____

HINT When adding a suffix that begins with a consonant to a root word ending in silent *e*, usually keep the *e*.

2. Robert's trumpet lessons are usually <u>noisey</u>.

_____

HINT When adding a suffix that begins with *-y* to a root word ending in silent *e*, usually drop the *e*.

3. Jake <u>hurryed</u> home to watch his favorite TV show.

_____

4. Joe was <u>hopeful</u> for the future.

_____

5. Dave was a bit <u>jumpy</u> at the dentist's office.

_____

6. There was much <u>sillyness</u> in the class when the mime performed.

_____

Lesson Practice

This passage contains mistakes. Use the Reading Guide to help you find the mistakes.

Reading Guide

What is the root word of *holding*?

How many words with prefixes do you see?

How many words have suffixes?

The Best Present Ever

(1) The best present I ever got was from my little brother, Mike. (2) When he was four years old, Mike had a lot of trouble <u>holding</u> a pencil and writing his name. (3) He used to get angry when people asked him to practice. (4) Sometimes the letters would come out upside down. (5) Other times he would write the letters going up in a line instead of across the page.

(6) My parents put me in charge of helping him to write. (7) We would practice every day, but he would <u>usualy</u> end up <u>unnhappy</u> with me. (8) <u>Finaly</u>, one day, I just gave up. (9) I told him I did not care if he never learned how to write his name. (10) Disappointed, Mike walked out of the room.

(11) Then the next day when I came home from school, I saw an envelope on my bed. (12) I opened it slowly and took out the <u>shiney</u> paper inside. (13) It was a paper with Mike's name written on it. (14) I could tell he had worked hard on writing his name. (15) The letters were crooked. (16) But to me they looked <u>beautiful</u>. (17) I felt such <u>happyness</u> and was so proud of Mike.

(18) "Sorry," he told me. (19) "Will you help me some more? (20) I won't get mad at you."

(21) "Of course," I said. (22) "You are doing a great job."

Answer the following questions.

1. What is the correct spelling of <u>finaly</u> in sentence 8?

   A. finalee

   B. finalay

   C. finally

   D. finnaly

2. Read sentence 7.

   We would practice every day, but he would <u>usualy</u> end up <u>unnhappy</u> with me.

   What is the correct way to spell <u>usualy</u> and <u>unnhappy</u>?

   A. usally, unhappy

   B. usualy, unhappy

   C. usually, unnhappy

   D. usually, unhappy

3. In sentence 16, the word <u>beautiful</u> means

   A. without beauty.

   B. full of beauty.

   C. the most beauty.

   D. before beauty.

4. Read sentence 17.

   I felt such <u>happyness</u> and was so proud of Mike.

   What is the correct way to spell <u>happyness</u>?

   A. happiness

   B. hapiness

   C. happieness

   D. hapyness

5. Write this sentence from the passage. Spell the underlined word correctly. Explain why you changed the spelling of the word.

   I opened it slowly and took out the <u>shiney</u> paper inside.

   _____

   _____

   _____

   _____

   _____

4 Synonyms, Antonyms, and Homophones

3.4.a, 3.4.b

 Getting the Idea

Synonyms are words that have the same or almost the same meanings. Here are some synonyms.

Word	Synonym
big	large, huge, enormous
difficult	hard, tough
fast	speedy, swift
good	great, excellent, fine, wonderful
pretty	beautiful, lovely

You can vary your writing and make it more interesting by using synonyms. Many synonyms have similar, but not exact, meanings. Read the sentences below.

Luke bought a *big* stuffed animal for the baby.
Luke bought a *huge* stuffed animal for the baby.
Luke bought an *enormous* stuffed animal for the baby.

Each sentence has a similar, but different, meaning. You must choose the synonym that makes the most sense in your sentence.

Antonyms are words that have opposite or almost opposite meanings. You can use antonyms to show how people, places, or things are different. Here are some antonyms.

Word	Antonym
big	small, little
difficult	easy, simple
fast	slow
good	bad, terrible
pretty	ugly

Sometimes, when you read sentences with antonyms, you can figure out the meaning of a new word. Read the sentences below.

> The dog's behavior was not <u>good</u> at all. In fact, it was <u>awful</u>.
> He ripped up the couch cushions and knocked over Mom's
> good vase. He's in a lot of trouble!

The words *good* and *awful* are antonyms. The sentences say that the dog was not good. He was awful. If you know the meaning of *good*, you can tell that *awful* means almost the opposite. The other details in the sentence help you to see that *awful* means "very bad."

Homophones are words that are pronounced the same but have different meanings. Homophones often have different spellings, too. Here are some homophones.

Word	Homophone
ate	eight
hear	here
know	no
rode	road
rose	rows
see	sea
to	too, two
wear	where

When you read, look at the spelling of words to make sure you understand their meaning. The word should make sense in the sentence. Read these two sentences.

> The man <u>rode</u> his horse to town.
> The <u>road</u> was wet and muddy.

The words *rode* and *road* sound the same. But they have different meanings. They are also spelled differently. In the first sentence, *rode* is the past tense of *ride*. In the second sentence, *road* is a path or highway.

Thinking It Through

Read the following paragraph, and then answer the question that follows.

Beth looked through the cabinet as her stomach growled. "Maybe a can of soup would be good," she thought to herself. She reached for some chicken noodle soup, opened it, and put it in a pot. Even if it wasn't the best soup she ever <u>eight</u>, she would no longer be hungry after <u>ate</u> o'clock.

Rewrite the last sentence using the underlined homophones correctly.

_____

_____

_____

_____

 Look at how the underlined words are spelled to figure out which words do not make sense in the sentence.

Coached Example

Read the passage and answer the questions.

Daniel could not hear his mother <u>angrily</u> yelling to him in the backyard. He had his music up too high. She furiously stomped out to the pile of leaves he was raking. But when she saw he was wearing headphones, she quickly knew what had happened. Her <u>frown</u> suddenly turned to a smile. She thought of how she could get his attention. Just as Daniel turned around, his mother jumped into the huge pile of leaves and threw some his way. Daniel jumped at first, and then happily burst into laughter. The two of them began throwing leaves at each other and laughing. Finally, Daniel turned down his music.

"Lunchtime," his mother said.

---

1. Which word in the passage is a synonym for <u>angrily</u>?

   A. furiously

   B. happily

   C. quickly

   D. suddenly

   HINT Remember that synonyms have similar meanings.

2. Which word in the passage is an antonym for <u>frown</u>?

   A. yelling

   B. attention

   C. smile

   D. laughter

   HINT Remember that antonyms are words with opposite meanings.

Lesson Practice

Use the Reading Guide to help you understand the passage.

Reading Guide

What is an antonym for *slowly*?

What is a synonym for *friends*?

Find the homophones in paragraph 9.

Pictures of the Sea

Alec and Lisa looked out the living room window at the moving truck next door. They wondered who would be moving into the big wood and stone house.

They hoped there would be someone their age for them to play with. As the movers <u>slowly</u> unloaded the truck, Alec and Lisa saw artists' easels. They saw large <u>paintings</u>. Some were painted <u>pale</u> blue and were pictures of the sea.

Just then, Alec's twin sister, Maya, entered the room. "What are you doing?" she asked.

"The new neighbors are moving in," Alec said. "Let's go see them. They look like artists."

Maya quickly <u>peered</u> out the window.

"All right," she said. "Maybe we can become <u>friends</u> with them." They told their parents where they were going and left for the front yard.

Just as they got to the edge of their yard, a boy about their age came toward them.

"Are you guys my new neighbors?" he asked.

"Yes," said Alec. "I see that someone in your family is an artist and likes to paint pictures of the sea. We love art," Alec added.

"I'm the artist," said the boy. "Perhaps we can do some art projects together." The kids started talking as if they had been pals forever.

Answer the following questions.

1. Which sentence from the passage has two homophones?

   A. "Maya quickly peered out the window."

   B. "They saw large paintings."

   C. "Just then, Alec's twin sister, Maya, entered the room."

   D. "They hoped there would be someone their age for them to play with."

2. What is a synonym for <u>paintings</u> in the passage?

   A. pictures

   B. easels

   C. projects

   D. artists

3. Read this sentence from the passage.

   Some were painted <u>pale</u> blue and were pictures of the sea.

   What is an antonym for <u>pale</u>?

   A. pail

   B. bright

   C. dull

   D. golden

4. Which two words from the passage are homophones?

   A. big, large

   B. would, wood

   C. neighbors, friends

   D. entered, left

5. Write this paragraph from the passage. Use synonyms so that the sentences have the same meaning as before.

   Alec and Lisa looked out the living room window at the moving truck next door. They wondered who would be moving into the big wood and stone house.

   _____

   _____

   _____

   _____

5 Meaning Clues, Structure Clues, and Phonetics

3.4.c

Getting the Idea

When you read, what do you do when you come across words, ideas, and information you do not know? You look for clues in the text. Knowing how to look for clues will help you make sense of what you read.

Meaning clues are words that help the reader understand the meaning of another word. Read the sentence below.

>The <u>tranquil</u> blue ocean calmed the sailors.

What does *tranquil* mean? Look at the other words in the sentence. They will give you clues to the meaning of the word. What would calm the sailors? The answer might be something peaceful. What can be peaceful? The blue ocean can be peaceful. By using the meaning clues in the sentence, you can figure out that *tranquil* means "peaceful."

Structure clues are punctuation marks or word arrangements that give hints about the meaning of a word or an idea. Structure clues may include words to compare or contrast. Words such as *like*, *and*, *both*, and *same* show how two or more things are alike. Words such as *unlike*, *while*, *however*, and *but* show how two or more things are different. Look at the paragraph below to see how clue words give hints about the meanings of words or ideas.

>Both mixtures and solutions combine things. In fact, anything you can combine is a mixture. For example, a cake is made up of a mixture of ingredients. A solution is also a mixture. Bleach and water is a solution. But unlike a mixture, which can be made up of solid objects, a solution will be made up of at least one liquid.

The paragraph compares mixtures and solutions. Look at the way the words *both* and *also* help you understand how mixtures and solutions are alike. Then look at the way the words *but* and *unlike* help you see how mixtures and solutions are different.

Phonetics refers to the way a word or word part sounds. You can use phonetics to help you pronounce, or say, words. Read the sentence below.

> There was a <u>pause</u> in the soccer game <u>because</u> it rained for
> a while.

Look at the words *pause* and *because*. If you don't know how to pronounce the word *pause*, look for other words in the sentence to give you phonetic clues. *Pause* and *because* have the same sound and are spelled the same way. This lets you know that the words rhyme. Phonetics can help you find the same vowel sounds in words. This will let you know how to pronounce, or say, a word.

Thinking It Through

Read the following paragraph, and then answer the question that follows.

Everyone who enters the <u>tournament</u> has to sign in at the front desk. The tournament will test your spelling abilities. The winner will receive an award that he or she will be proud of. Remember to enter the tournament if you feel you are a great speller!

Which clues in the paragraph help you know that a <u>tournament</u> is a competition or a contest?

_____

_____

_____

_____

_____

 HINT   First, underline the meaning clues that help you decide the meaning of the word.

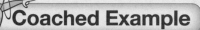

Coached Example

Read the passage and answer the questions.

In 1918, Virginia <u>adopted</u> the American dogwood as its state flower. Why do states like to have a flower to call their <u>own</u>? A state flower gives people something to be proud of. People from Virginia feel a sense of pride when they see a dogwood. It also brings people together. State flowers also have another purpose. They can help people become interested in the history of their state.

---

1. Which words from the passage help you find the meaning of <u>adopted</u>?

   A. to call their own

   B. something to be proud of

   C. sense of pride

   D. brings people together

   HINT Use meaning clues to help you find the meaning of the word.

2. Read this sentence from the passage.

   Why do states like to have a flower to call their <u>own</u>?

   Which word has the same vowel sound as <u>own</u>?

   A. lean

   B. clown

   C. rain

   D. stone

   HINT Use phonetics to look for the word that rhymes with *own*.

Lesson Practice

Use the Reading Guide to help you understand the passage.

Reading Guide

Which word in paragraph 1 has the same final vowel sound as *garage*?

What clue in paragraph 3 helps you figure out the meaning of *appearance*?

How can you tell what a hawk is by using meaning clues?

Hiding Out

An animal that wears <u>camouflage</u> is like an animal wearing a costume. Chameleons, some toads, fish, and insects all hide by using this trick of nature.

How do animals with camouflage hide? A chameleon will blend into its <u>surroundings</u>. It will begin to look like the trees, bark, or rocks around it. The color and pattern of its skin will change. Soon, it will completely blend in with its background.

Why do these animals change their <u>appearance</u>? They change the way they look so that they can stay safe from <u>predators</u>. Because these animals want to eat them, animals use camouflage to try to stay safe. Instead of finding an animal to eat, the predator will see only leaves, trees, or grass.

Like a chameleon, a toad also uses camouflage. But a toad uses camouflage to look like a rock. It will sit on a rocky surface. Its body will turn shades of brown. A <u>hawk</u> will have a hard time seeing it. The bird will look for a meal someplace else.

A chemical in some animals' bodies allows them to use camouflage. It is a trick of nature reserved for special types of animals to let them stay safe and <u>survive</u> in the wild.

Answer the following questions.

1. Which words from the passage help you to know the meaning of <u>camouflage</u>?

   A. like an animal wearing a costume

   B. sit on a rocky surface

   C. shades of brown

   D. a toad also uses camouflage

2. Which words from the passage help you to know the meaning of <u>predators</u>?

   A. to look like a rock

   B. will see only leaves, trees, or grass

   C. Because these animals want to eat them

   D. this trick of nature

3. Which paragraph uses structure clues to compare and contrast a chameleon and a toad?

   A. paragraph 1

   B. paragraph 2

   C. paragraph 3

   D. paragraph 4

4. Which words in the last sentence of the passage help you know what <u>survive</u> means?

   A. trick of nature

   B. special types of animals

   C. stay safe

   D. in the wild

5. Which clues from the passage help you know the meaning of <u>surroundings</u>?

   _____

   _____

   _____

   _____

   _____

   _____

6 Context Clues

3.4.d

Getting the Idea

As you read, you may come across a word you do not know. Look for clues in the other words in the sentence or in nearby sentences to help you figure out the meaning of an unfamiliar word. These clues are called **context clues**. Here are the different kinds of context clues.

A **definition** gives the exact meaning of a word. Sometimes commas are placed around the definition. Read the sentence below.

Please do not <u>utter</u>, or say, a single word.

The definition of the word *utter* is shown right in the sentence. It means "say."

A **restatement** is another way to say the same thing. Often, it is a sentence. Read the sentence below.

The coach was <u>delighted</u> that his team won. He was very pleased.

Context clues help you figure out the meaning of the word *delighted*. The words *very pleased* in the second sentence restate how the coach felt.

An **example** is a specific type of something. A peach is an example of a fruit. Now read the sentence below.

The students played different <u>instruments</u>, such as the trumpet, flute, and violin.

The words *trumpet*, *flute*, and *violin* are examples of instruments. They help you understand what the word *instruments* means.

Cause and effect shows how one event causes another event to happen. A **cause** is the reason something happens. An **effect** is what happens as a result of a cause. Words such as *because, so,* and *as a result* are clues that signal cause and effect. Read this sentence.

> Donna slept late, so she was <u>tardy</u> for school.

> <u>Cause</u>: Donna slept late.
> <u>Effect</u>: She was <u>tardy</u> for school.

Sleeping late can cause someone to be late. Being tardy is the effect. So *tardy* means "late."

Synonyms are words that have the same or almost the same meanings. Using synonyms to figure out the meaning of a word is a lot like using the definition. Look at this example.

> The star gave off a beautiful <u>glimmer</u>, or shine.

If you do not know what *glimmer* means, you can find a clue in the sentence. *Glimmer* means almost the same as *shine*.

Antonyms are words that have opposite or almost opposite meanings. Look for clue words such as *not* or *instead of* to see when antonyms are being used. Read this example.

> Instead of being thrilled about the news, they were <u>upset</u>.

If people are not thrilled about something, they may feel upset. So *upset* means "not being thrilled."

Compare and contrast shows how two or more people or things are alike and how they are different. To **compare** means to show how things are alike. Look for clue words such as *like* or *and* to compare. To **contrast** means to show how things are different. Look for clue words such as *unlike* or *but* to contrast. Read the example below.

> Ed is <u>hilarious</u>, just like that very funny actor on television.

Ed is being compared to an actor who is very funny. So, *hilarious* means "very funny."

Thinking It Through

Read the following paragraph, and then answer the questions that follow.

Darren heard the wind <u>rustle</u>, or shake, the leaves on the trees outside. He wondered if the storm was already on its way. It was not supposed to be here until tomorrow morning. Darren pulled the covers over his head and waited to hear the sound of the thunder.

What does the word <u>rustle</u> mean? What clues in the passage help you figure out the meaning?

_____

_____

_____

_____

_____

HINT   The comma and the word *or* can be a clue that the writer is trying to say something in another way.

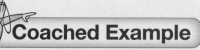

Coached Example

Read the passage and answer the questions.

Maggie finished her homework as quickly as she could. She could not stop thinking about her favorite television show. She knew if she finished her homework, she would be able to sit down and watch it.

The grandfather clock in the living room began to chime. It was eight o'clock. Maggie ran into the kitchen. She grabbed some popcorn to enjoy during the show.

She <u>bounded</u> down the stairs and rushed into the family room. She turned on the television set. Soon, the picture appeared on the screen. But Maggie was <u>disappointed</u>. She felt let down. There was a baseball game on instead of her favorite show!

---

1. Which sentence tells the meaning of the word <u>disappointed</u>?

   A. "Soon, the picture appeared on the screen."

   B. "She could not stop thinking about her favorite television show."

   C. "She felt let down."

   D. "There was a baseball game on instead of her favorite show!"

   HINT Think about how the words or sentences around the word *disappointed* can help you understand what it means.

2. What does the word <u>bounded</u> mean in the passage?

   A. appeared

   B. screamed

   C. walked

   D. ran

   HINT Look for the word that is a synonym for *bounded*.

Lesson Practice

Use the Reading Guide to help you understand the passage.

Reading Guide

Think about the meaning of *endless*. Is the distance from Maine to Georgia a long or short distance?

Look for clue words to help you figure out the meaning of *snake* as it is used in paragraph 1.

Which word in paragraph 4 is defined with a synonym?

The Appalachian Trail

Would you like to take a hike through the eastern part of the United States? It would take a long time, wouldn't it? Yes, but it would be worth it! The Appalachian Trail is a hiking trail that seems <u>endless</u>. It goes all the way from Maine to Georgia. It is the longest trail in the United Sates. It is about 2,179 miles long and <u>snakes</u> through fourteen states.

The path goes through the state parks and local forests. Different hiking clubs help to <u>maintain</u> the trail in their state. They keep the trail in good condition.

The idea of the Appalachian Trail was thought of in 1921 by a man named Benton MacKay. Over the years, many volunteers have helped to clear the path. The trail was finally <u>completed</u> in 1937.

If you wanted to walk the entire length of this <u>extensive</u> trail, it would take a very long time. People <u>estimate</u>, or guess, that it would take 5 million footsteps to walk the trail. That's a lot of hiking! But people are <u>welcome</u> to enjoy the trail. They are invited to hike the trail at their own pace. One quarter of the Appalachian Trail lies in Virginia. That's 550 miles, including the 20 miles that border Virginia and West Virginia.

Answer the following questions.

1. What kind of context clue helps you figure out the meaning of <u>maintain</u> in paragraph 2?

   A. restatement

   B. cause and effect

   C. compare and contrast

   D. example

2. What is the meaning of <u>extensive</u> in paragraph 4?

   A. thick

   B. short

   C. long

   D. thin

3. What is the meaning of <u>completed</u> in paragraph 3?

   A. started

   B. finished

   C. changed

   D. revised

4. What does the word <u>estimate</u> mean in paragraph 4?

   A. volunteer

   B. guess

   C. welcome

   D. try

5. Read this sentence from the passage.

   But people are <u>welcome</u> to enjoy the trail.

   What is the meaning of <u>welcome</u>? Which sentence helped you figure out the meaning of the word?

   _____

   _____

   _____

   _____

   _____

7 Content Area Vocabulary

3.4.e, 3.4.f

Getting the Idea

When you read texts that give information, pay attention to the kinds of words that are used. These words do not include everyday language. You would probably not use these words in a conversation with a friend. For example, in a social studies textbook, you might learn about where a country is located, based on latitude and longitude. However, you would not use the words *latitude* and *longitude* to tell someone how to get to the store.

The language, or words, you read will change depending on the **content area**. A content area is a subject of study, such as science, math, or social studies. Music and art are also content areas. Each content area uses words that have meanings that are special to that subject. When you read in a content area, you will come across words you do not know. These unfamiliar words are usually in bold (or dark) print. Often, these words appear in a glossary at the end of the text. A **glossary** is a list of words and their meanings. You will learn more about a glossary in the next lesson.

Sometimes, you will come across a word that you know but that is being used differently. This may happen because one word can have many meanings. Think about the word *pound*. When you read a science book, the word *pound* might be used to tell how much something weighs. But when you read a social studies book, the word *pound* might mean the money used in England.

Read the two passages below.

Ant Colonies

Many people raise ant <u>colonies</u> as a hobby. An ant colony is an underground place where a group of ants live, breathe, and eat. These colonies have underground rooms that are connected by small tunnels. For example, there are rooms for nurseries and food storage. These colonies are built by worker ants.

The Original Thirteen Colonies

The original thirteen <u>colonies</u> were founded by British settlers. Although the colonies were all along the Atlantic Ocean, there were New England Colonies, Middle Colonies, and Southern Colonies. However, the colonies joined together during the American Revolution. Later, the original thirteen colonies became the United States of America.

The two passages are different, both in content area and in language. The first passage is from a science article. It talks about ant colonies. The second passage is from a social studies textbook. It talks about the original thirteen colonies. Notice that the word *colonies* is used differently in the passages. In the first passage, *colonies* means the places where ants live. In the second passage, the *colonies* were the original thirteen English settlements. As you can see, the same word can have different meanings and uses in different content (or subject) areas.

Even an English language arts book uses its own special vocabulary. For example, in a language arts book, you can learn about *capitalization*, *punctuation*, *nouns*, *pronouns*, *verbs*, *adjectives*, *adverbs*, *subjects*, and *predicates*.

Thinking It Through

Read the following paragraph, and then answer the questions that follow.

Economics is the study of how people choose to use resources. Many economic choices involve goods and services. **Goods** are items that people buy or sell, such as a book, a car, or a computer. **Services** include work done for other people for a fee. Doctors, lawyers, teachers, and chefs all provide services.

Why are some words in bold (or dark) print? In which content area would you study these words?

_____

_____

_____

_____

_____

HINT In which content area would you learn about history, government, and economics?

Coached Example

Read the passage and answer the questions.

If you hold a ball with your hand and drop it, it falls to the ground. The force of gravity acts on the ball. <u>Gravity</u> is the force that pulls two <u>objects</u> toward each other. The force of gravity acts on all objects on Earth. All objects are pulled toward Earth's center. Without gravity, everything on Earth would float away. Gravity holds Earth in its orbit around the sun, too. Without gravity, Earth would not travel around the sun.

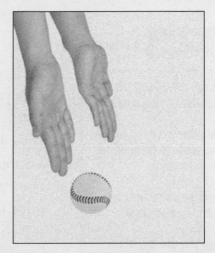

1. What does the word <u>gravity</u> mean?

   A. the pull of Earth

   B. the pull of one object on another

   C. the force of Earth

   D. the force of the sun

    Find the word *gravity* in the passage. Then find the words in the sentence that tell what *gravity* means.

2. What does the word <u>objects</u> mean as it is used in this passage?

   A. disagrees

   B. words that receive the actions of verbs

   C. things

   D. goals or purposes

   HINT Replace the word *objects* with each answer choice in the sentence. Which makes sense?

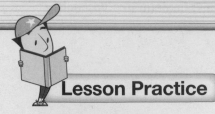

Lesson Practice

Use the Reading Guide to help you understand the passage.

Reading Guide

How are the underlined words used in the passage?

What other words would make sense in place of the underlined words?

In which content area would you find this passage?

Would you use any of the underlined words in an everyday conversation with a friend?

The Articles of Confederation

In 1777, Congress approved a plan for a new nation. This plan was called the Articles of Confederation. The states, however, did not <u>ratify</u>, or approve, the Articles until 1781. From 1781 until 1789, the Articles of Confederation served as the new nation's constitution. The Articles were important because they expressed the colonies' wish to become a country.

There were several weaknesses in the Articles of Confederation, however. The document created a group of states, or <u>confederation</u>, rather than one government. States kept most of the power and authority.

By 1786, it was clear that the Articles needed to be revised or replaced. Many colonial leaders believed that the United States needed a stronger national government. James Madison of Virginia and other <u>delegates</u>, or representatives, met at the Constitutional Convention in Philadelphia in 1787.

For months, the delegates worked to write a new constitution. They agreed that the country would continue to be a republic. In a <u>republic</u>, citizens elect their government leaders to carry out their wishes. The delegates also agreed that the new constitution would be the highest law of the land. The constitution limited the power of each branch of government. For example, the president had the power to <u>veto</u>, or cancel, any bill passed by Congress.

Answer the following questions.

1. What does the word <u>ratify</u> mean?

   A. approve

   B. disapprove

   C. join together

   D. write

2. According to the passage, <u>confederation</u> means

   A. a nation.

   B. a document.

   C. a group of states.

   D. a government.

3. In paragraph 3, the word <u>delegates</u> means

   A. replacements.

   B. presidents.

   C. constitutions.

   D. representatives.

4. What does the word <u>veto</u> mean?

   A. agree

   B. elect

   C. pass

   D. cancel

5. What is a <u>republic</u>? Which words help you to understand its meaning?

_____

_____

_____

_____

_____

_____

_____

_____

8 Using a Dictionary, Thesaurus, and Glossary

3.4.g

Getting the Idea

A **dictionary** is a book or an online source that gives the definition (or meaning) of a word. The **definition** tells what a word means. A dictionary can be a book or it can be online. Words in a dictionary are listed alphabetically (in ABC order). When you look up a word in a dictionary, you will see

- how to pronounce, or say, the word.
- where the word comes from and its root.
- the part of speech of the word (such as *noun* or *verb*).
- the different meanings of the word.

Look at this entry from a children's dictionary:

> **change** (chaynj) 1. *verb* to put or take in place of something else. 2. *verb* to make or become different. 3. *noun* small coins. 4. *noun* another set of clothes

The part in parentheses shows you how to pronounce the word. Look at the part of speech. It tells you whether the word is a verb or a noun, or can be used as both. Look at the numbers. This entry shows that the word *change* has four meanings.

A **glossary** is a list of words and their meanings. You can often find a glossary at the back of a nonfiction book. A glossary is like a dictionary. The words are listed in alphabetical (or ABC) order. In a glossary, the meaning of the word is given. Some glossaries may also tell you how to pronounce, or say, the word.

A glossary does not list every word used in the book. It lists only important words that the reader may not know. These words are shown in bold print in the main text. A glossary will give only the meaning of a word as it is used in the book.

Look at the following glossary entries from a science book.

> **bird** warm-blooded animal with feathers, wings, and a beak
> **mammal** warm-blooded animal with hair or fur
> **reptile** cold-blooded animal with dry, scaly skin

Remember: If you are reading a book and don't understand what a word means, you can turn to the glossary at the back of the book. If the glossary does not have the word you are looking for, look up the word in a dictionary.

A **thesaurus** is a book or an online source that gives synonyms and antonyms for words. Like a dictionary and a glossary, a thesaurus lists words in alphabetical (or ABC) order. After each word, a list of synonyms, or words with similar meanings, is given. Antonyms, or words with opposite or almost opposite meanings, are given after the list of synonyms. Suppose you wanted to find some synonyms and antonyms for the word *big*. The thesaurus entry might look like this:

> **big**
> SYN: large, huge, great, enormous, gigantic
> ANT: small, little, tiny, petite, undersized, slight

The word in bold print is the word you are looking up. The synonyms are shown below it. Then, the antonyms are listed.

You can vary your writing by using a thesaurus. If you are using the same word over and over again, a thesaurus can help you find a similar word to use. The synonym you choose, however, must make sense in the sentence. For example, suppose you wanted to replace the word *big* in the sentence below.

Our book sale made a <u>big</u> profit this summer.

It would not make sense to replace *big* with *enormous* in this sentence unless you made a lot of money. But the word *large* would make sense. Remember: The word you choose must make sense in the sentence.

Thinking It Through

Read the following glossary entries, and then answer the question that follows.

American Revolution the Revolutionary War (1775–1783) that was fought by the American colonies to gain independence from Great Britain

colony an area that is under the control of a country in another place

Great Britain an area that ruled the American colonies before the American Revolution

tax money given to a government by its people to help pay for government services

Explain how you can tell where in this glossary the word <u>patriot</u> would appear.

_____

_____

_____

_____

HINT Think about how glossary entries are listed.

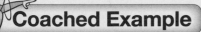

Coached Example

Read the dictionary entry and answer the questions.

spring (spring) 1. *noun* a season of the year that comes after winter. 2. *noun* a place where water or oil shoots up from the ground. 3. *noun* a coil of metal that returns to its original shape after being pushed together or pulled apart. 4. *verb* to jump into action suddenly

1. Read this sentence.

   The dog will <u>spring</u> into action as soon as he sees his treat.

   Which is the correct meaning of the word <u>spring</u> as it is used in the sentence?

   A. meaning 1

   B. meaning 2

   C. meaning 3

   D. meaning 4

   HINT Think about the part of speech of *spring* as it is used in the sentence.

2. Read this sentence.

   I can't wait to plant a garden this <u>spring</u>.

   Which meaning of the word <u>spring</u> is used in the sentence?

   A. meaning 1

   B. meaning 2

   C. meaning 3

   D. meaning 4

   HINT Review each meaning to see which one makes the most sense in the sentence.

Lesson Practice

Use the Reading Guide to help you understand the passage.

Reading Guide

Where can you look to find the meaning of *invention*?

How can you find a synonym for the word *important*?

Which word in paragraph 4 would you likely find in the glossary of a book about Benjamin Franklin?

Poor Richard's Almanack

Benjamin Franklin is known for his <u>bright</u> ideas and interesting <u>inventions</u>. In 1732, he came up with the clever idea to publish a newspaper. He called the paper *Poor Richard's Almanack*. He hoped that the *Almanack* would be a useful guide for the American colonists.

Franklin did not want people to know that he was the author of the *Almanack*. So, he wrote the paper under the name of Richard Saunders. He thought that by using another name, he would have more <u>freedom</u> as a writer.

Franklin's paper included many features that helped to <u>educate</u> the colonists. For example, it had weather <u>forecasts</u> for the year. These forecasts were <u>important</u> for farmers and travelers. It also contained a calendar, poems, news stories, and wise sayings.

Many of Franklin's wise sayings, or proverbs, were about <u>saving</u> money and staying healthy. Some proverbs from *Poor Richard's Almanack* live on today. One famous proverb we still use is "Early to bed and early to rise, makes a man healthy, wealthy, and wise."

Poor Richard's Almanack continued to be printed every year until 1757. People came to expect reading about Poor Richard and looked forward to getting their paper. Sometimes, it was the only thing that the colonists bought all year.

Today, *Poor Richard's Almanack* is still important because it tells us so much about early American history.

Answer the following questions.

1. Which is the correct meaning for the word <u>bright</u> in paragraph 1?

    A. giving out light

    B. clear

    C. smart

    D. lively

2. Which antonym would you find in a thesaurus for the word <u>saving</u>?

    A. change

    B. spending

    C. saying

    D. keeping

3. Which synonym would you find in a thesaurus for the word <u>educate</u>?

    A. ask

    B. almanac

    C. paper

    D. teach

4. Read this sentence from the passage.

    For example, it had weather <u>forecasts</u> for the year.

    Where could you find the meaning of the underlined word if it were not in a glossary?

    A. dictionary

    B. thesaurus

    C. almanac

    D. magazine

5. Suppose you want to find the meaning of <u>freedom</u>. Where would you look for the meaning of the word? Explain your answer.

    _____

    _____

    _____

    _____

    _____

1 Review

Read the passage and answer the questions that follow.

Thomas Edison, American Inventor

Would you like to invent things to make life easier? What would you make? A man named Thomas Edison spent his entire life inventing new things. In fact, his inventions changed the way people lived.

Edison was born in Ohio in 1847. He was the seventh child in his family. His family moved to Michigan when Edison was seven years old.

Edison did not spend much time at school. His father had a very large library where the young Edison was able to study. Edison's mother taught him at home.

At the age of twelve, Edison sold candy and newspapers on trains. He then taught himself how to print his own newspapers. While working on trains, Edison did chemical experiments. He was also good with machines. As he got older, he got a job as a telegraph operator. Edison liked working at night so that he could read and experiment. One night in 1867, he spilled acid onto the floor. The acid dripped between the floorboards and onto his boss's desk below. The next morning Edison was fired.

But Edison would continue to invent. One of his earliest inventions was the fire alarm. He improved the telegraph, too. Edison sold his clever inventions. He used the money to build a laboratory where he could do research. His laboratory had machines, electricity, and other brilliant inventors.

One of Edison's most famous discoveries, or inventions, was how to record sound. The machine he invented was called a phonograph.

Some people would say that his greatest discovery was the lightbulb. However, Edison did not invent the first electric lightbulb. In England, Joseph Swan started the research for modern lightbulbs. But his bulb needed too much energy and didn't last long. Edison and his workers discovered a new way of making lightbulbs work longer.

Thomas Edison died in 1931 at the age of 84. By the end of his life, he had made 1,093 inventions. His brilliant inventions transformed, or changed, the world.

1. Read this sentence from the passage.

   Edison sold his inventions.

   Which word in the sentence has the long *o* sound?

   A. Edison

   B. sold

   C. his

   D. inventions

2. How many syllables are in the word <u>floorboards</u> from paragraph 4?

   A. 1

   B. 2

   C. 3

   D. 4

3. Read this sentence from the passage.

   Some people would say that his greatest <u>discovery</u> was the lightbulb.

   What is the root word in the word <u>discovery</u>?

   A. disc

   B. dis

   C. cover

   D. discovery

4. Which words from paragraph 5 are homophones?

   A. clever, brilliant

   B. inventions, machines

   C. to, too

   D. could, would

5. Which word from paragraph 5 is a meaning clue for <u>laboratory</u>?

   A. inventions

   B. machines

   C. electricity

   D. research

6. Read this sentence from the passage.

   The next morning Edison was <u>fired</u>.

   Which word is an antonym for <u>fired</u>?

   A. trained

   B. hired

   C. worked

   D. changed

7. Read this sentence from the passage.

   His brilliant inventions <u>transformed</u>, or changed, the world.

   Which context clue helped you figure out the meaning of <u>transformed</u>?

   A. inventions

   B. changed

   C. world

   D. brilliant

8. Based on paragraph 4, how do you know that acid is a liquid?

   A. It dripped between the floorboards.

   B. Edison experimented with it.

   C. Edison was fired.

   D. It was on his boss's desk.

9. Which word from the passage would MOST LIKELY be found in a book about a scientist?

   A. money

   B. laboratory

   C. modern

   D. improve

10. Which is the BEST dictionary definition of <u>telegraph</u>?

   A. a system for sending messages a long distance across a wire

   B. a way to change how messages are sent

   C. a message watched on a screen

   D. a system for receiving messages only

Read the passage and answer the questions that follow.

"Peter Breaks Through"

excerpted and adapted from Peter and Wendy
by J. M. Barrie

Occasionally, in her travels through her children's minds, Mrs. Darling found things she could not understand. Of these, the most puzzling was the word *Peter*. She knew of no Peter. Yet he was here and there in John's and Michael's minds, and especially in Wendy's.

"But who is he, my pet?" Mrs. Darling asked Wendy.

"He is Peter Pan, Mother."

At first, Mrs. Darling didn't know what to think. After thinking back into her childhood, she did remember a Peter Pan. There were <u>strange</u> stories about him. She had believed in him at the time. But now that she was married and full of sense, she <u>certainly</u> doubted whether there was any such person.

"Besides," she said to Wendy, "he would be grown up by this time."

"Oh no, he isn't grown up," Wendy said. "And he is just my size."

Mrs. Darling spoke with Mr. Darling, but he just smiled. "<u>Mark</u> my words," he said, "it is some <u>nonsense</u> Nana has been putting into their heads. It is the sort of idea a dog would have. Leave it alone, and it will blow over."

But it would not blow over, and one morning Wendy made a startling discovery. Some leaves had been found on the nursery floor. They had not been there when the children went to bed. Mrs. Darling was puzzling over them when Wendy said with a smile:

"I do believe it is that Peter again!"

"Whatever do you mean, Wendy?"

"It is so <u>naughty</u> of him not to clean up," Wendy spoke out, showing her dislike for bad behavior. She was a <u>tidy</u> child, thought Mrs. Darling, while Peter was not neat at all.

Wendy explained in quite a matter-of-fact way that she thought Peter sometimes came to the nursery in the night.

"What nonsense you talk, for such a nice, level-headed child. No one can get into the house without knocking," Mrs. Darling told Wendy.

"I think he comes in by the window," Wendy replied.

It was quite true. The leaves had been found very near the window.

Mrs. Darling did not know what to think. It all seemed so natural to Wendy. You could not dismiss it by saying she had been dreaming.

11. Which word from the passage has a short *e* sound?

    A. pet

    B. leaves

    C. stories

    D. Pan

12. Which word from the passage has the most syllables?

    A. certainly

    B. behavior

    C. Occasionally

    D. discovery

13. What does the prefix mean in the word <u>nonsense</u>?

    A. again

    B. before

    C. full of

    D. not

14. Read this sentence from the passage.

    At first, Mrs. Darling didn't know what to think.

    Which word in the sentence is a homophone?

    A. did

    B. think

    C. know

    D. first

15. Which word is a synonym for <u>certainly</u>?

    A. puzzling

    B. tolerant

    C. sometimes

    D. definitely

16. Read this sentence from the passage.

> **"It is so <u>naughty</u> of him not to clean up," Wendy spoke out, showing her dislike for bad behavior.**

Which words from the sentence help you figure out the meaning of <u>naughty</u>?

A. spoke out

B. clean up

C. dislike for

D. bad behavior

17. Read this sentence from the passage.

> **She was a <u>tidy</u> child, thought Mrs. Darling, while Peter was not neat at all.**

Which part of the sentence helps you figure out the meaning of <u>tidy</u>?

A. She was a tidy child

B. thought Mrs. Darling

C. while Peter was not neat

D. at all

18. Which word in the passage would MOST LIKELY be found in a science book?

A. stories

B. discovery

C. remembered

D. nonsense

19. Where would you look to find a list of synonyms for the word <u>strange</u>?

A. thesaurus

B. dictionary

C. glossary

D. encyclopedia

20. Read this sentence from the passage.

> **"<u>Mark</u> my words," he said.**

Which is the correct meaning of <u>mark</u> as it is used in the sentence?

A. to notice

B. to grade or score

C. a symbol or stamp

D. to check off

CHAPTER

2 Reading Comprehension

Lesson 9 Fiction and Nonfiction
3.5.a, 3.5.e, 3.5.i, 3.6.a, 3.6.k

Lesson 10 Ask and Answer Questions
3.5.f, 3.6.d

Lesson 11 Main Idea and Supporting Details
3.5.i–k, 3.6.f–h, 3.6.j

Lesson 12 Compare and Contrast
3.5.d, 3.6.i

Lesson 13 Problem and Solution
3.5.h

Lesson 14 Predictions
3.5.c

Lesson 15 Make Inferences and Draw Conclusions
3.5.b, 3.5.g, 3.6.b, 3.6.e

Lesson 16 Text Features
3.6.c, 3.7.b

Chapter 2 Review

9 Fiction and Nonfiction

3.5.a, 3.5.e, 3.5.i, 3.6.a, 3.6.k

Getting the Idea

Before you read something, think about your purpose for reading it. For example, you might read a story to be entertained. You might read a science magazine or a book about history to get information. Whatever you read, it is important to know why you are reading it. This is called **setting a purpose** for reading. Setting a purpose for reading helps you focus on *what* you are reading and *why* you are reading it.

Just as you set a purpose for reading, an author sets a purpose for writing. An **author's purpose** is the reason an author writes something. An author's purpose is to entertain, to inform, or to persuade readers. Read the passage below.

> "Stop following me around," Rabbit told Fox. "I will share my meal with you, but I will not *be* your meal."
> "OK," said Fox. "Let's eat something together!"

This passage is an example of fiction. It uses animal characters and dialogue. **Dialogue** is the words the characters say to each other. The author's purpose for writing this passage it is to **entertain**, or amuse, the reader. Your purpose for reading it is to have fun. Writing that entertains is usually fiction.

Fiction is writing that describes imaginary people, places, and events. A story is a good example of fiction. Stories have imaginary characters that can be people or animals and made-up settings and events. A story has a beginning, a middle, and an end. **Fairy tales**, **fables**, and **folktales** are examples of fiction.

Poetry is fiction, too. Although poetry can be about real or made-up people and ideas, all poetry has a rhythm, or beat. Many poems also have words that rhyme, or have the same end sound. Unlike stories, poems are written in lines, not in sentences that make up paragraphs. Poetry uses creative language. Like a story, a poem is an example of fiction.

Now read an example of nonfiction.

> A bird is an interesting animal. It has wings and feathers. All birds hatch from eggs, but not all birds can fly.

This example gives the reader information about birds. The author's purpose in writing it is to use facts to **inform** the reader or **audience**. You often read nonfiction to get information. You may also read it to learn how to do something step by step.

Nonfiction is writing that gives facts and information to the reader. **Facts** can be proved to be true. Nonfiction writing is about real people, places, things, and events. A textbook and a science or history book are examples of nonfiction. Newspaper or magazine articles, a diary, a letter, or a how-to book are also nonfiction. Biographies and autobiographies are nonfiction, too. A **biography** is a true story about a person's life, written by someone else. An **autobiography** is a true story about a person's life, written by that person.

Now read this advertisement.

> Come to our sale on Saturday to get the lowest prices of the year! There is no sale like ours. Our deals will make you smile.

The author's purpose in writing this ad is to persuade. When an author's purpose is to **persuade**, the author tries to get the audience to agree with his or her opinion. An **opinion** is a statement that is usually based on the author's feelings or beliefs. It is not based on facts. Writers usually use nonfiction writing to persuade.

It is useful to know if what you are reading is fiction or nonfiction. This will help you set your purpose for reading. It will also help you discover the author's purpose for writing.

Thinking It Through

Read the following poem, and then answer the question that follows.

Thanks to the founders of our country!
Thanks to the red, white, and blue.
You have made this country great,
And my feelings for you are true!

What is the author's purpose in writing this poem?

_____

_____

_____

HINT Think about how the poem makes you feel. Is it fun to read? Why?

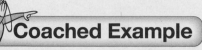

Coached Example

Read the passage and answer the questions.

Dear Mr. Layton,

We hope you will listen to our request. We have gone to this school for three years. We have seen the school playground equipment become worn and broken. We think that the playground is becoming dangerous. We do not want our classmates to get hurt while they are playing.

Please think about getting new equipment. We think it is important to fix up the playground for the safety of the students.

Perhaps you could send someone to our class to talk to us about this problem.

Sincerely,
Mrs. Rivera's Class

---

1. What is the author's purpose in writing the letter?

   A. to entertain

   B. to persuade

   C. to inform

   D. to explain

   HINT Think about what the letter asks Mr. Layton to do.

2. Why is this letter an example of nonfiction writing?

   A. It has imaginary characters.

   B. It tells a make-believe story.

   C. It explains how to make something.

   D. It gives facts about real life.

   HINT Review the meaning of nonfiction. Does the letter use facts and tell about real people and things?

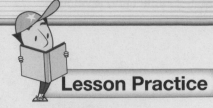

Lesson Practice

Use the Reading Guide to help you understand the passage.

Reading Guide

What is your purpose for reading this passage?

What kind of writing usually has characters?

Look through the passage for real people and facts. Are there any?

The Gift

Jason went into his parents' bedroom to find the socks he had left on the floor. As he reached down to pick up his socks, he noticed a shiny red box under his parents' bed. "What's this?" wondered Jason as he knelt down on the floor. He reached under the bed and pulled out the box. The note on the package was addressed to him. It said, "Congratulations!" It was from Mom and Dad. Jason thought long and hard. He wondered what he had done to deserve a present.

"What's taking you so long?" Jason's mother asked as she walked into the bedroom. She stopped in her tracks. "Oh, you found your gift," she said with a nod.

"Mom, what did I do?" he asked. "Why am I being congratulated?"

"Why don't you open your gift to find out?" she said.

Jason ripped open the wrapping paper and tore open the box. It was a T-shirt. He picked it up. It said, "I'm a big brother!"

"Your father and I are adopting a new baby," his mother said. "You're going to be a big brother!"

"Yes!" Jason cried with excitement. "Congratulations to me!"

Answer the following questions.

1. What kind of writing is the passage?

   A. poetry

   B. fiction

   C. nonfiction

   D. advertisement

2. What is the author's purpose for writing the passage?

   A. to ask a question

   B. to persuade the reader

   C. to entertain the reader

   D. to give the reader true information

3. What clues in the passage helped you figure out the author's purpose?

   A. The passage tells how to make something.

   B. The passage uses facts to give information.

   C. The passage tries to get the reader to agree with the author.

   D. The passage has characters, dialogue, and made-up events.

4. In what kind of book would you MOST LIKELY find this passage?

   A. a textbook

   B. a book of poetry

   C. a book of short stories

   D. a book of fables

5. Suppose Jason wanted to write a letter telling his friends about becoming a new big brother. What might his purpose be for writing?

   _____

   _____

   _____

   _____

10 Ask and Answer Questions

3.5.f, 3.6.d

Getting the Idea

Fiction is writing that describes made-up people, places, and events. When you read fiction, you should ask yourself questions. The questions you will ask are called *who*, *what*, *where*, *when*, *why*, and *how* questions.

Look at the list below of some questions to ask yourself when you read. Suppose you are reading a story. These questions will help you better understand the characters, the setting (where and when the story takes place), and the events.

- Who is the story about?
- Where does the story take place?
- When does the story take place?
- What happens in the story?
- Why did the author write the story?
- What is the problem in the story?
- How is the problem solved?

Read the passage below. Think about what questions you would ask yourself as you read. Often the answers are right in the text!

Kevin had never flown in a plane before. Last week was his first time flying. Kevin was flying to Norfolk, Virginia, to visit his grandmother. He was nervous. When the plane started to shake, Kevin became scared. He looked around at the other passengers. Nobody else looked afraid. The captain talked over the loudspeaker. He told everyone not to worry. The shaking was normal. Kevin relaxed. The rest of the trip was fine.

Here are some questions you might ask yourself about the story. Also read the answers in the chart.

Who is this story about?	Kevin
Where does the story take place?	in an airplane
When does it take place?	last week
What happens in the story?	Kevin is nervous about flying for the first time.
Why is Kevin scared?	The plane begins to shake.
How is the problem solved?	The captain says that the shaking is normal.

The passage you have just read is fiction. Now read this nonfiction passage. Think about the questions you would ask yourself as you read.

In 1860, a man named William Hepburn Russell came up with the idea of a mail service. It was called the Pony Express. The Pony Express riders rode on horseback across the western part of the United States to deliver mail. People in California were able to get mail from people in Missouri in only ten days. Before that, the quickest way to deliver mail was by stagecoach. Stagecoaches went from Missouri to Texas, and then on to California. The trip by stagecoach took about 25 days.

Who is the paragraph about?	William Hepburn Russell
What is the paragraph about?	the Pony Express
What does the picture show?	a Pony Express rider
Why did Russell start the Pony Express?	to deliver mail more quickly

Thinking It Through

Read the following paragraphs, and then answer the question that follows.

Eight U.S. presidents have come from Virginia. Only one of them has not lived in the White House. That was George Washington. Although Washington helped to plan the White House, he never got to live and work in it. He left office before the White House was finished.

The White House was built between 1792 and 1800. It has 132 rooms. The president's office in the White House is called the Oval Office. Today, the president and his family live and work in the White House.

Write three questions about the passage.

_____

_____

_____

_____

_____

HINT   Think of questions that begin with *who, what, when, where,* and *how.*

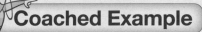

Coached Example

Read the passage and answer the questions.

Forgetful Nicole

Nicole was walking home from school. She noticed that her backpack felt lighter than usual. At first, she didn't pay much attention. The day was too beautiful, and she was happy to be done with school for the day. However, she soon started thinking about her homework. She needed to study math. She also wanted to start thinking about her science project.

She suddenly stopped. Uh-oh! She looked inside her backpack. She had forgotten her math book! She ran back to school, but the doors were locked. She would have to wait until tomorrow.

---

1. Based on the title above the passage, this passage will be about

   A. Nicole's forgetfulness.

   B. Nicole's best qualities.

   C. Nicole's science project.

   D. Nicole's walk home.

   HINT Pay careful attention to the information in the title. How is Nicole described?

2. Which question is answered by the passage?

   A. Who locked the school doors?

   B. What did Nicole forget?

   C. Where is Nicole's school?

   D. When did Nicole get out of school?

   HINT The answer is often written right in the passage.

Lesson Practice

Use the Reading Guide to help you understand the passage.

Reading Guide

What does the title tell you about the passage?

Where do koalas live?

What kind of question can you ask yourself as you read paragraph 2?

The Koala

Have you ever heard someone call a <u>koala</u> a *koala bear*? Perhaps it's because koalas look like cute teddy bears. However, they aren't members of the bear family at all. Koalas are actually members of a group of animals called <u>*marsupials*</u>. A marsupial is an animal that has a pouch for carrying its young. Many kinds of marsupials, such as koalas and kangaroos, live in Australia.

A mother koala gives birth to one baby a year. The newborn koala is called a *joey*. A joey is about as big as a large jelly bean! At first, it stays and sleeps in its mother's pouch and drinks her milk. However, after a few months, it leaves the pouch and climbs on its mother's back. What do koalas eat? They love to eat the leaves of eucalyptus trees.

Often people are tempted to reach out and touch koalas because they look so cute and cuddly. However, doing that is dangerous. Do not try to pet koalas! They are wild animals and have very sharp claws. Koalas also have strong arm and shoulder muscles. These muscles help them climb and jump from tree to tree.

Answer the following questions.

1. Which is the MOST IMPORTANT question to ask yourself as you read?

    A. What are koalas?

    B. How many kinds of marsupials are there in the world?

    C. Where can I find eucalyptus trees?

    D. When do koalas climb trees?

2. According to the passage, you should NOT pet koalas because

    A. they climb trees.

    B. they are marsupials.

    C. they are cute and cuddly.

    D. they have sharp claws.

3. Which of the following questions was answered in the passage?

    A. Why does a joey climb on its mother's back?

    B. How long are a koala's claws?

    C. Where do newborns sleep?

    D. When do koalas sleep?

4. Which of the following questions was NOT answered in the passage?

    A. How big is a joey?

    B. When do koalas eat?

    C. What do koalas eat?

    D. Why are koalas dangerous?

5. According to the passage, what are marsupials?

    _____

    _____

    _____

    _____

    _____

    _____

    _____

11 Main Idea and Supporting Details

3.5.i–k, 3.6.f–h, 3.6.j

Getting the Idea

The **main idea** of a passage is the most important point the author wants the reader to understand. You can usually figure out the main idea by asking yourself, "What is this passage mostly about?" Sometimes the author puts the main idea in the first or last sentence of a passage. The author might even put the main idea in the title. Then, the title will give you a clue as to what the passage is about.

Supporting details give information about the main idea. Supporting details can be facts, examples, descriptions, quotations, dates, names, or places. These details support, or back up, the main idea. Read this passage.

> In colonial America, most people learned only what they needed to know to survive. For men, this often meant learning a trade, such as making shoes. For women, this meant learning to cook, sew, and raise children. Children went to school for only a few years just to learn the basics. The basics were reading, writing, and arithmetic. Today, most Americans stay in school at least through high school. Many students go on to college.

You can use a diagram to find the main idea and supporting details in a passage. The diagram on the next page shows the main idea and details in the passage above.

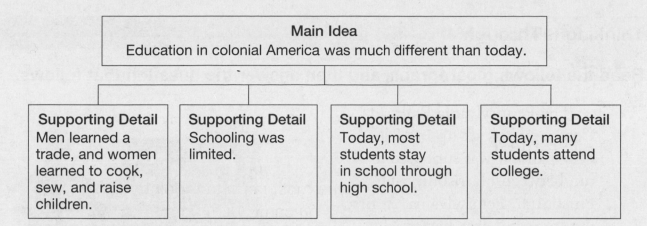

You can also skim, scan, and summarize to find the main idea. When you **skim**, you read a passage quickly to get the general idea. You may read the title and headings, the first and last paragraph, or just the first sentence of each paragraph. When you **scan**, you look for key words or terms to help you find specific information. Scanning is useful for finding dates, names, and places. You can also **summarize** to state the main idea. When you summarize, you tell only the most important information from what you have read.

When you read for information, it is important to find the main idea and supporting details. Read the passage below.

> Mark Twain is one of our most interesting writers. His real name was Samuel Clemens. He was born in Missouri in 1835. Missouri fought with the South during the Civil War. When he was a teen, Twain left Missouri and worked as a printer. He wrote *The Adventures of Huckleberry Finn* and *The Adventures of Tom Sawyer*.

What is the main idea of the passage? Mark Twain is one of our most interesting writers. Which details support the main idea? Mark Twain's real name was Samuel Clemens. He was born in Missouri in 1835. He left home as a teen and worked as a printer. He wrote *The Adventures of Huckleberry Finn* and *The Adventures of Tom Sawyer*.

Reread the fourth sentence in the paragraph. Does it support the main idea? No. The paragraph is about Mark Twain, not about Missouri.

When you read, ask yourself these questions about the passage. They will help you find the main idea and supporting details.

- What is the passage mostly about?
- Which details support the main idea?

Thinking It Through

Read the following paragraph, and then answer the question that follows.

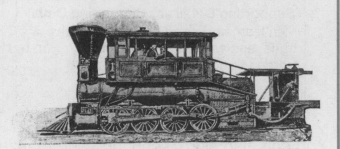

The Pennsylvania Railroad Company was set up in 1846. Originally, it was supposed to run between Harrisburg and Pittsburgh, Pennsylvania. At first, the company only had freight trains. These trains carried goods and supplies. Then, in 1848, it began running a passenger train. As a result of this service, the company grew quickly. By 1856, the Pennsylvania Railroad went to Chicago, Illinois. After the Civil War, it went to Washington, D.C.; St. Louis, Missouri; New York City; and other large cities. By 1910, its railroad tracks covered 10,000 miles. Today, the Norfolk Southern Railway owns most of the Pennsylvania Railroad.

What is the main idea of this paragraph?

_____

_____

_____

_____

HINT The main idea is what the passage is mostly about.

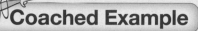

Coached Example

Read the passage and answer the questions.

It would be Jessica's birthday in just three days. She checked her birthday guest list again and again. She couldn't wait for her party. She knew that her friends would have a great time at the bowling alley, where they would all meet.

"Did you see the weather report?" her dad asked as he entered the kitchen. "It looks as if you might have a birthday blizzard this year."

"Oh, no!" cried Jessica. Her heart sank. The winter weather was the worst part of having a birthday in January. She knew that her friends' parents would not be driving them to the bowling alley during a blizzard. She put her birthday list away.

"We'll just have to wait and see," she said patiently. She looked out the kitchen window and crossed her fingers. All she could do was hope for the best.

---

1. What is the passage MOSTLY about?

   A. Jessica's dad

   B. bowling

   C. Jessica's birthday

   D. Jessica's friends

   HINT Read the passage again. Look at each answer choice. What does the author want you to know?

2. Which detail can you find by skimming the passage?

   A. which friends Jessica has invited

   B. how old Jessica will be

   C. how Jessica's dad feels about her being a year older

   D. when Jessica's party will be

   HINT Some of these choices are not in the passage. Skim the passage to see which answer you can find.

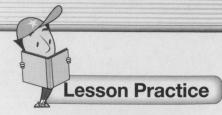

Use the Reading Guide to help you understand the passage.

Reading Guide

What is paragraph 1 mostly about?

What is paragraph 2 mostly about?

Which details support the idea that bald uakaris stand out from other monkeys?

The Bald Uakari

There are many kinds of monkeys all over the world. Some monkeys are called New World monkeys. These monkeys live in Central and South America. They live in the tropics because they need to stay warm. They have long tails and flat, wide noses.

There are about 100 species of New World monkeys. One of these is called the bald uakari. The uakari is a little over two and a half feet long, including its tail. Uakaris weigh from about six and a half pounds to seven and a half pounds. They have long, fluffy hair. Their hair ranges in color from white to orange-red.

Bald uakaris stand out from other monkeys. In fact, many people think these monkeys look strange. So what is so odd about these monkeys' appearance? Uakaris have bright red faces. The color is so vivid that they look as if they are suffering from a bad sunburn! Even though they have a lot of hair on their bodies, they have little or no fur on their faces. This makes them look even stranger. When a uakari's face is pale, it may mean it is sick. A bright red face is a sign of good health.

Uakaris search for food in groups of about ten. It could be that searching for food in groups helps them search larger areas. Uakaris like to eat fruit, leaves, insects, and seeds.

Answer the following questions.

1. What is the main idea of the passage?

   A. New World monkeys are different from Old World monkeys.

   B. Bald uakaris are interesting animals.

   C. Central and South America are home to many monkeys.

   D. Monkeys eat many different kinds of food.

2. What is paragraph 3 MOSTLY about?

   A. what the bald uakari eats

   B. where the bald uakari lives

   C. what the bald uakari looks like

   D. how the bald uakari searches for food

3. Which of the following is NOT a supporting detail from this passage?

   A. The uakaris have bright red faces.

   B. A bright red face is a sign of good health.

   C. The uakari is a little over two and a half feet long.

   D. Uakaris live in trees in groups of about ten.

4. According to the passage, uakaris like to eat

   A. fruit, fish, and seeds.

   B. fruit, leaves, insects, and seeds.

   C. leaves, fruit, and vegetables.

   D. seeds, leaves, insects, and fish.

5. According to the passage, what makes the bald uakari stand out from other monkeys?

   _____

   _____

   _____

   _____

   _____

12 Compare and Contrast

3.5.d, 3.6.i

Getting the Idea

To **compare** people or things is to tell how they are alike. To **contrast** people or things is to tell how they are different. Readers often **compare and contrast** characters, settings, and events. They also compare and contrast kinds of writing. The kinds of writing might be **fiction** and **nonfiction**. They might be two types of fiction, such as a story and a play. They might also be two types of nonfiction, such as a **biography** and an **autobiography**. Read the two passages below. Look for how the passages are alike and how they are different.

Andrew the Artist

Andrew was a very good artist. He spent all his free time painting. Andrew painted before school, after school, and during the weekend. He drew large pictures of fruit. Andrew didn't have many friends. He liked spending his time painting in his room.

Maria the Athlete

I am the captain of my swim team. All of my teammates look up to me. I always try to encourage everyone to work hard. Swimming has become an important part of my life. I practice every day. My team is the best in the city. I think of myself as being outgoing. I have many friends.

The first passage is about Andrew, but it is written by someone else. The second passage is about Maria, and it is written by her. Both passages are nonfiction. They tell about real people and true events. However, the two people are different. So is the type of writing. The passage about Andrew is a brief biography. The passage about Maria is a brief autobiography.

A biography tells the true story of a person's life, but it is written by another person. A biography uses the **third-person point of view**. The narrator uses *he* or *she* to tell about the person. An autobiography tells the true story of a person's life, too, but it is written by that person. An autobiography uses the **first-person point of view**. The narrator tells his or her own story by using *I*.

Ask yourself these questions about the two passages.

- How are Andrew and Maria alike?
- How are they different?

Both Andrew and Maria are hard workers. They are also both good at what they do. Andrew is creative. Maria is athletic. Maria has a lot of friends and likes to spend time with them. Andrew doesn't have many friends and likes to paint alone in his room.

Readers can compare and contrast kinds of writing. They can also compare and contrast the setting in two different stories. The **setting** tells where and when the story takes place. Read these examples.

Burning Desert

The blazing sun beat down on the red desert sand. For miles, there was nothing but sand and dry desert brush. The wind blew hard every now and again, kicking up dust and sending the brush tumbling.

Full Moon, Empty Town

A crumpled brown bag blew in the wind. Down the cold, empty street, a street lamp flickered and buzzed in the night. All the windows were dark and boarded up. Behind the empty brick building, the full moon began to rise.

How are the two settings alike? How are they different? Both the desert and the town have no people. It is day in the desert and night in the town. The weather is sunny, hot, and dry in the desert. It is cold and windy in the town.

Readers can also compare and contrast the plot in different stories. The **plot** is the sequence of events in the beginning, middle, and end of a story. Readers can also compare and contrast characters in the same story. The **characters** are the made-up people or animals that the author tells us about. Comparing and contrasting the setting, the plot, and the characters will help a reader better understand a story.

Thinking It Through

Read the following paragraph, and then answer the questions that follow.

Mona and her twin sister, Liza, like to go to the library on a rainy afternoon. At the library, Mona always goes straight to the magazines. She likes reading about her favorite movie stars. Liza always goes straight to the poetry books. Then, they both sit down at a table together and read while the rain falls outside.

How are the sisters alike? How are they different?

_____

_____

_____

_____

_____

HINT   Look for similarities and differences before answering the question.

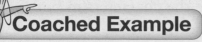

Coached Example

Read the passages and answer the questions.

The Bat Cave

Steve and Tom walked slowly into the dark cave. Tom pointed his flashlight into the darkness. Suddenly, a large, black bat flew straight toward the two boys. Tom panicked and dropped his flashlight. The boys listened as the flashlight tumbled down the rocks and splashed into some water. Steve fumbled for his flashlight in total darkness.

Steve's knees shook as he reached into his backpack. Finally, he found the flashlight. He pointed the flashlight deep into the cave. Then, he flashed it quickly back to Tom. He could tell by Tom's face that it was time to head back outside.

Blackout!

Geraldine sat in her living room and read her book. Outside, the storm grew stronger. The raindrops sounded like pebbles tossed against the window. Thunder shook the house. Suddenly, the lights flickered and went out. Geraldine got up from her chair and walked slowly in the dark. She opened all the drawers in the kitchen, searching for the flashlight.

Geraldine found the flashlight. But when she turned it on, the bulb was so dim that she could barely see in front of her. Geraldine calmly looked around the kitchen for candles and matches.

1. How are the characters in both passages alike?

   A. They are all in a cave.

   B. They are all afraid of bats.

   C. They all like to read books.

   D. They are all in the dark.

   HINT Compare the characters to see how they are the same and where they are.

2. How are the characters in both passages different?

   A. Steve and Tom are scared, but Geraldine is calm.

   B. Steve and Geraldine are calm, but Tom is scared.

   C. Steve and Tom are calm, but Geraldine is scared.

   D. Geraldine and Tom are scared, but Steve is calm.

   HINT Which character is different from the other two characters?

3. How are the two passages different?

   _____

   _____

   _____

   _____

   _____

   _____

   _____

   _____

   _____

   HINT Think about the characters, settings, and events.

Lesson Practice

Use the Reading Guide to help you understand the passages.

Reading Guide

Was the passage written by Rosa Parks, or was it written by someone else?

What does the passage tell the reader about Rosa Parks?

How is this passage like other passages you have read about people and events from real life?

Rosa Parks, an American Hero

Rosa Parks has been called heroic, strong, and determined. Do you know why? She did something amazing on December 1, 1955. It happened in Montgomery, Alabama. Rosa Parks, who was African American, was riding a city bus. She sat in a seat in a row reserved for African Americans. At the time, African Americans were made to sit in the back of the bus. An African American always had to give up his or her seat to a white passenger. Like many people, Rosa Parks thought this law was unfair.

The bus driver told Parks to get up and give her seat to one of the white passengers. When she refused, she was arrested. After that, thousands of people stopped riding buses in Montgomery. This was called a boycott. The bus boycott went on for months. It became news around the country. On November 13, 1956, the United States Supreme Court ruled that buses could not separate people on the basis of race. Rosa Parks had won!

Rosa Parks may have been an ordinary woman from Alabama, but she did something extraordinary. She helped make an important difference in our country!

Mr. Lee, Teacher and Friend

Was the passage written by Mr. Lee, or was it written by someone else?

What does the passage tell the reader about Mr. Lee?

How is this passage and the one about Rosa Parks alike? How are they different?

When I first got my job teaching at Lincoln Elementary School, I was a little bit nervous. I had never taught children before. I had just graduated from college. Although I was a little nervous, I was also very excited.

I will always remember my first class of students. They were so filled with energy and excitement for learning. Even today I try to remember what it was like to teach those children for the first time. I remember one student named George. He thought it was unfair that the third graders could not have their own science fair. He wanted the third graders to be able to have a science fair just like the fourth graders.

I helped George to ask the school principal about the science fair. I thought it was important that the students learn as much as they could in school.

The principal agreed to let the third graders have a science fair. George's hard work had paid off. Even now I try to help my students as much as I can. I try to be their teacher as well as their friend. Sometimes students end up learning more than they ever thought they would. I think teachers do, too!

Answer the following questions.

1. Which passage is an autobiography?

   A "Rosa Parks, an American Hero"

   B. "Mr. Lee, Teacher and Friend"

   C. both passages

   D. neither passage

2. How were Rosa Parks and Mr. Lee alike?

   A. They were both teachers.

   B. They were both famous.

   C. They both stood up for what they believed in.

   D. They both worked to change the laws of the United States.

3. How was Rosa Parks different from Mr. Lee?

   A. She refused to follow a law or rule.

   B. She enjoyed teaching children.

   C. She wanted to help third graders.

   D. She worked hard.

4. Both passage are about

   A. people.

   B. children.

   C. schools.

   D. buses.

5. What is the difference between a biography and an autobiography?

   _____

   _____

   _____

   _____

   _____

   _____

13 Problem and Solution

3.5.h

Getting the Idea

A story has characters, a setting, and a plot. The **characters** are the imaginary people or animals in the story. The **setting** is where and when the story takes place. The **plot** tells the events, or what happens in the story. Usually, the author tells the events in the order in which they happened, from first to last.

The plot of a story has a beginning, a middle, and an end. Usually, the author presents a problem at the beginning of the story. The **problem** is also called the **conflict**. Usually, the main character has to solve the problem, or conflict, before the end of the story. As the character works through the problem, he or she learns something important.

Sometimes a story has more than one problem. Read the passage below.

> John was late for work again. He rushed to put on his hat and coat. Then he opened the front door. To his surprise, snow was piled high everywhere. The snow must have fallen during the night. What would he do? He would surely be late for work now!

John has a problem. He is late for work again. Then his problem gets even bigger. There is a lot of snow on the ground. Now it will take him even longer to get to work. He will have to shovel the snow from the driveway and drive to work slowly on the snowy roads.

The **solution** is the way the problem, or conflict, is solved in a story.

Read the rest of the story about John to find out how his problem is solved.

> After John had been shoveling his driveway for ten minutes, he heard his cell phone ring in his pocket. He answered the phone. It was his boss. She told him to stay at home today. The office would be closed because of the snowy weather. John's problem was solved. He did not have to worry about being late for work again. But today he had learned a good lesson. From now on, he would wake up earlier on workdays.

The solution to John's problem is that the office will be closed because of the bad weather. But the problem has taught John a lesson. From now on, he will get up earlier for work. The **problem and solution** in a story helps to organize the events. The problem sets up the story. The solution brings the story to its **resolution**, or end.

Stories have different kinds of problems, or conflicts. The conflict may be within a person (or character). It may be between two people. Or it may be between a person and an outside force such as nature. Here is a simple way to look at these three types of conflicts.

- person against self
- person against person
- person against nature

Let's see how these conflicts work in the passage you have read. At first, the story about John is an example of person against self. John's conflict is within himself. He is having trouble getting to work on time. Then the story becomes a conflict between person and nature. John's problem is now with the snowy weather. Suppose John had a conflict with his boss. That would be an example of a person against person conflict.

Thinking It Through

Read the following paragraph, and then answer the question that follows.

Zelda the Zebra looked up at her mom sadly.

"Why can't I play with the other zebras?" she asked.

But Zelda knew the answer. She was in trouble for being mean to her little brother. Now her mother would not let her play with the other zebras for two days. Zelda frowned. She had never had such a problem before.

What is the problem, or conflict, in the paragraph?

_____

_____

_____

_____

HINT   Think about who Zelda's conflict is with.

Coached Example

Read the passage and answer the questions.

Evan's stomach growled. He reached up to the counter for an apple. He stretched and stretched, but he couldn't reach the fruit. He knew he was not allowed to climb on chairs. But he did not know how else to get the apple. He pushed the kitchen chair slowly toward the counter. The scraping of the chair made a loud noise on the floor.

Just then, Dad came into the kitchen. "What are you doing, Buddy?" he asked.

"I can't reach the apple up there," said Evan.

"You know you shouldn't climb on chairs," said his dad. He handed Evan the apple. "Next time, just ask."

1. What is Evan's problem in the story?

   A. He doesn't want to eat an apple.

   B. He is hungry but can't reach the apple.

   C. He wants to climb on a chair.

   D. There are no apples to eat in the house.

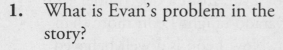 The problem is the conflict that the character is having.

2. How is Evan's problem solved?

   A. Evan climbs on a chair and gets the apple.

   B. Evan decides to eat something else.

   C. Evan's dad gets the apple for him.

   D. Evan's mom picks him up so he can reach the apple.

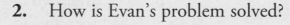 The solution is how the character's problem is solved.

Lesson Practice

Use the Reading Guide to help you understand the passage.

Reading Guide

Characters solve problems in stories. Who are the characters in this story?

Who has a problem in this story?

How does the character solve the problem?

My Dog Leon

They say that if you want a friend, get a dog. Whoever said that never met Leon. Leon has always been the worst dog in the world. He never listens. He rips up everything, from the morning paper to my slippers. I guess he isn't such a good friend.

Last night, I was getting ready for bed. Suddenly, Leon knocked down a glass from the kitchen table. Dad had to spend half an hour cleaning up the broken glass. Dad told me, "Brian, if Leon doesn't start behaving, we will have to get rid of him." The very next day, I put up a large sign at the community center. It read: "Dog Trainer Needed!"

After two days, we got a call from a dog trainer who had seen the ad. Mr. Alvarado taught Leon more than we could have hoped for. Now Leon is a well-behaved dog. I was so happy when Dad said, "Brian, it's okay. Leon can stay."

Answer the following questions.

1. What is the problem in the story?

   A Leon does not behave.

   B. Leon does not want to live in the house.

   C. Dad does not like dogs.

   D. Brian can't find a dog trainer.

2. How does Brian try to solve the problem?

   A. He gets a dog trainer for Leon.

   B. His father changes his mind about Leon before the dog trainer arrives.

   C. Mr. Alvarado persuades Brian's dad to keep the dog.

   D. Brian runs away with the dog.

3. How is the problem solved?

   A. Dad cleans up the broken glass.

   B. Dad learns to train Leon.

   C. Leon gets to stay because he learns to behave.

   D. Leon runs away.

4. What would the conflict be if Brian didn't like the dog trainer?

   A. person against nature

   B. person against person

   C. person against self

   D. It cannot be known.

5. Tell the events that led to the solution in the story. Give the events in order.

   _____

   _____

   _____

   _____

   _____

   _____

14 Predictions

3.5.c

Getting the Idea

A **prediction** is a guess about what might happen in the future. You probably make predictions all the time. You may predict the weather for tomorrow. You may predict whether your team will win the next game.

When you read a story, you also make predictions. For example, you may predict what a character will say or do next. As you read, ask yourself, "What is most likely to happen next?" Sometimes, you can make a prediction about the most important events in a story even before you read. You can look at the title of the story to give you a hint. You can also page through the story to look at the pictures. Pictures help to tell a story. They can help you predict what a story will be about. Read this first part of the passage below.

> Tracy's family was planning their summer vacation. Her parents had asked her sister, her brother, and her for their vacation ideas. Tracy had said she would love to return to Virginia Beach. The family had gone there two years ago, and she could still remember the sand castles she had built with her sister. Her birthday was also in July, and a trip to Virginia Beach would make a nice birthday present. But her mother was saying they had just been there two years ago. Her father was suggesting Washington, D.C. Tracy said that Washington, D.C., was too hot in the summer. Just then, her father said, "It's time to decide. Let's take a vote."

Predict what will happen next in the story. Up to this point, we don't know what her sister and brother will decide. Will the family return to Virginia Beach? Will they go somewhere else on their vacation? What clues help you predict what will happen in the story?

As you read the rest of the story, see if the events turned out as you predicted. If you guessed right, you can **confirm** your prediction in the story. If your prediction does not seem to be correct, you can **revise** it as you read. This means you can change your prediction. Now read the rest of the passage to find out what happens in the story.

> Tracy's dad handed out five folded slips of paper. The family voted. Tracy's dad read the first vote. It was for Virginia Beach. Then, he read the next vote. It was the same: Virginia Beach. After that, he read the next two votes. They were for Washington, D.C. The votes were now even: two to two. Tracy's dad opened the last piece of paper. "We're going to Virginia Beach!" he cried. He seemed so happy about it that Tracy wondered if he had voted for Virginia Beach after all.

If you predicted that the family would vote for Virginia Beach, you can confirm your prediction. However, if you predicted that the family would not be going there, your prediction would have been wrong. Of course, you may have revised your prediction before you finished reading the story. You may have changed your mind based on what the author tells you or on what you already know from your own experiences.

As you read, take the time to see where the story is going. Think about what you have learned about the characters. Consider the new events in the story. Did you expect them to happen? Then make a prediction. Ask yourself: What will happen next in the story? How will the story end?

Thinking It Through

Read the following paragraph, and then answer the questions that follow.

Ali felt ready for the game. He and his team had been practicing all season for the championship. For the past month, it had been nothing but school, baseball practice, and homework. Everything was riding on this game. He was hoping his team would win. Ali did several practice throws and hit the ball a few times. He felt pretty good. The other players looked fine. What could go wrong?

How do you predict the game will turn out? What clues from the story helped you make your prediction?

_____

_____

_____

_____

HINT   Read the paragraph again. How does Ali think his team will do in the championship game?

Coached Example

Read the passage and answer the questions.

Mrs. Diaz looked at every street sign she passed. "I know the building is around here somewhere," she said.

"Mom, we're late," said Kari. "I thought you had directions."

"I do," said Mrs. Diaz. "It's just that the street name on my directions is not here."

"There it is!" yelled Kari, pointing to the next street sign. "Miami Drive."

"Oh, great!" said Mrs. Diaz. "Thank you, sweetheart." She sighed. "We're still five minutes late, though. I hope the ballet did not start without you!"

"I think they'll wait," replied Kari. "After all, I am the star ballerina in the show. We just have to hurry!"

---

1. What do you predict will happen when Kari arrives at the performance?

   A. The performance will be over.

   B. The performance will be canceled.

   C. The performance will not have started without Kari.

   D. There will be no one inside the building.

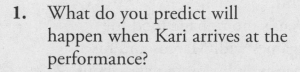 Think about the most likely thing that will happen. Base your prediction on what you have already read.

2. Kari will MOST LIKELY

   A. forget how to dance.

   B. change her mind about performing.

   C. give a great performance.

   D. go to the wrong building to perform.

HINT What do you learn about Kari in the story? How does she feel about getting to the performance? This will help you make a prediction about what might happen next in the story.

Lesson Practice

Use the Reading Guide to help you understand the passage.

Reading Guide

Think about what might happen next in the story.

A prediction is a guess you make about the future. What prediction can you make about the storm?

What prediction can you make about Marcus?

The Storm

Marcus was ready for the storm. He had listened to the weather report two days before. He knew a hurricane might be hitting the area. He worked with his dad to make the house ready. They nailed boards over the windows. They moved outdoor furniture that could blow away. They also packed clothes so they could leave in a hurry.

Marcus and his family knew they should be out of their town by noon. They got into their car at eight in the morning and headed to Grandma's house. She lived two hours away from the storm's path.

When they got to Grandma's house, they watched the news. It seemed that the storm was slowing down. But the storm would still be very strong. They were glad they had made it to Grandma's early to get her house ready if the storm did hit.

Grandma and Marcus's mom made food for everyone. Dad played games with Marcus and his brother. They waited patiently for more news about the storm.

Late that night, Marcus was in bed in Grandma's guest bedroom. He said goodnight to everyone. He would have to wait until morning to hear more news about the storm.

Answer the following questions.

1. What will MOST LIKELY happen in the morning?

   A. The storm will not have arrived.

   B. Marcus will hear about the storm.

   C. The storm will have changed direction.

   D. There will be no TV reports about the storm.

2. When do you think Marcus's family will return to their home?

   A. in the middle of the night

   B. in the middle of the storm

   C. when the storm is over

   D. after the storm cleanup is done in a few weeks

3. Who will likely return to Marcus's house after the storm?

   A. his entire family

   B. just Marcus

   C. just his mother

   D. just his brother

4. What will MOST LIKELY happen when the family is back home again?

   A. The family will go on vacation.

   B. The family will drive back to Grandma's house.

   C. Marcus and his dad will take down the nailed boards from the windows.

   D. Marcus and his dad will finish the game they started at Grandma's house.

5. What do you think will happen in the story? What makes you think so?

   _____

   _____

   _____

   _____

   _____

15 Make Inferences and Draw Conclusions

3.5.b, 3.5.g, 3.6.b, 3.6.e

Getting the Idea

Sometimes an author doesn't tell you everything about a character. You may need to figure out the character for yourself. You have to make an inference about why the character acts in a certain way or what the character is really like. When you make an **inference**, you make a good guess about someone or something. You use what the author tells you and what you already know from your own reading and experiences to make an inference.

You make inferences *while* you read. You draw conclusions about the inferences you made *after* you read. When you draw a **conclusion**, you use the inferences you made during reading to make a decision about what you have read. Sometimes you draw conclusions about a character or a situation in a story. Other times, you draw conclusions about the entire story. For example, if a character in a story cries, you can make the inference that the character is upset. After you read, you may draw the conclusion that the character is an unhappy person. You may even draw the conclusion that the author wanted to write a sad story.

Use clues to make inferences and then draw conclusions. A character's words and actions are clues that can help you make inferences while you read. Look at this example.

Words from Passage	Inference and Conclusion
The boy smiled as he looked at his math test score.	The boy got a good grade on his math test. The boy is proud of himself.

Making inferences and drawing conclusions can help you better understand what you read. Now read the following poem.

> The sun went away.
> The clouds came out to play.
> Plop! Plop! Plop!
> The leaves on the trees will soon drop.

If you made the inference that it has started to rain, you are correct. You can draw conclusions about the poem by using what the speaker tells you and what you already know about rain and the seasons. For example, you might draw the conclusion that the poem takes place in the early fall because the leaves on the trees will soon drop. Or you might draw the conclusion that it is raining so hard that the leaves will drop from the heavy rain.

You can also draw conclusions as you read nonfiction. Use the evidence from the text and what you already know to learn more as you read. Now read the paragraph below.

> When many people hear the name Mount Vernon, they think of the home of George Washington. This large, lovely home, which is near Alexandria, Virginia, has become a National Historic Landmark. So beautiful are the gardens that people visit Mount Vernon just to see them. In fact, Mount Vernon is one of the most popular stops for tourists in the United States.

You can make the inference that Mount Vernon is a beautiful place to visit. You can draw the conclusion that many people think it is important to protect the house.

Thinking It Through

Read the following poem, and then answer the question that follows.

Every book is my friend.
Ask me what I want to do today.
First, I want to read.
Then, I want to play.

What conclusion can you draw about the person speaking in the poem?

_____

_____

_____

_____

HINT   Think about what the speaker says and wants to do. This will help you draw a conclusion about the person speaking in the poem.

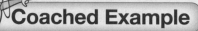

Coached Example

Read the passage and answer the questions.

Everyone knows that Thomas Jefferson is an important person in Virginia history. But did you know that he also started the University of Virginia? In 1819, Jefferson decided that the new nation needed a new kind of school. The university was the first of its kind not to be linked to any religious or political group. The school was also the first to allow students to choose the classes they wanted to take.

The University of Virginia opened in 1825. It had just eight teachers and sixty-eight students. Today, many universities around the world use the same ideas that Jefferson had back in the 1800s.

1. Why do you think Jefferson started the University of Virginia?

   A. He always wanted to be a teacher.

   B. He wanted everyone to be able to become president.

   C. He was angry at teachers of other schools.

   D. He loved the new country and wanted its people to get a new kind of education.

   HINT Think about what you already know about Thomas Jefferson and schools. Then choose the answer that makes the most sense.

2. Why do many universities still use Jefferson's ideas?

   A. Jefferson forced everyone to follow his ideas.

   B. The school was successful.

   C. People liked Thomas Jefferson.

   D. People thought the government wanted them to use Jefferson's ideas.

   HINT Think about how people learn today. Then think about why people might like to learn in this way.

Lesson Practice

Use the Reading Guide to help you understand the passage.

Reading Guide

Read paragraphs 1–4 carefully. How does Mrs. Lew act toward Mimi? Can you make the inference that Mrs. Lew is Mimi's mother?

Use what the author tells you in paragraphs 2 and 3 and what you already know. What inference can you make about the play Mimi is in?

What conclusions can you draw about Mimi's plans for a career in the future?

After the Show

Mrs. Lew met Mimi by the stage door. She was holding some flowers for her. When Mimi appeared, Mrs. Lew could see the big smile on her face.

"You did it!" shouted Mrs. Lew. "You overcame your fears! You made an excellent Dorothy in the play."

"And did you see the dog? She was such a great Toto!" cried Mimi with excitement. "I was afraid to work on stage with a dog. You never know what a dog will do!"

Mrs. Lew hugged Mimi and gave her the flowers. "Let's go backstage," said Mimi.

Backstage, Mrs. Lew met the other actors and the director. She was very proud of her daughter and her hard work. "Everyone did a wonderful job," Mrs. Lew told the others.

"Thanks, Mrs. Lew!" they all said.

Then Mimi and her mother sat down with the director. "What do you think about Mimi's idea to go to acting school this summer? She wants to do the best she can in every show," added Mrs. Lew.

The director looked at them both. "That would be a great idea if that's what Mimi really wants to do," he said. "What do you think, Mimi?"

"I think there is nothing I would want more," she said.

Answer the following questions.

1. How did Mimi do in the play?

   A. She did a good job.

   B. She did a poor job.

   C. She forgot her lines.

   D. She is not sure how she did.

2. Why does Mrs. Lew give Mimi flowers after the show?

   A. She is angry with Mimi.

   B. She is proud of Mimi.

   C. That is what you do after a show.

   D. Mrs. Lew was told by the director to bring the flowers.

3. Which clue tells the reader that Mrs. Lew supports Mimi's acting?

   A. She says hello to the other actors.

   B. She says hello to the director.

   C. She asks the director about Mimi's idea to go to acting school.

   D. She hugs Mimi.

4. In paragraph 1, what clues tell the reader that Mimi is proud of herself?

   A. Mrs. Lew has flowers for Mimi.

   B. Mrs. Lew stands by the stage door.

   C. Mimi meets Mrs. Lew at the stage door.

   D. Mimi has a big smile on her face.

5. How did you choose your answer to the last question? Give one clue from the passage that supports your answer to question 4.

   _____

   _____

   _____

   _____

16 Text Features

3.6.c, 3.7.b

Getting the Idea

Writers use text features to organize and explain information in a text. Text features also help readers find information. **Text features** include the title, headings, table of contents, index, and captions. A **caption** is a short title or description that usually comes below a picture and tells what the picture is about. Unusual or interesting print is another example of a text feature. **Bold** (or dark) **print**, italics (slanted type), and highlighting can draw the reader's attention to a word or section in a text.

A **title** is the name of a book, story, article, poem, play, or another type of writing. The title can give a hint as to what the writing is about. It can help readers decide if they want to read the book, for example. Look at the titles of these three books.

Abraham Lincoln   *My Dad Is Great*   *All About Goldfish*

Which one would you like to read?

Headings are words that name what a section in a passage or book is about. Headings introduce readers to what they are about to read. They also help readers follow the information. Headings are usually written in bold (or dark) print and are like a title. Look at the headings below.

Lincoln's Early Life
Lincoln's School Days
Lincoln as President
Lincoln and the War

A **table of contents** is a text feature in the front of a book. It shows the name of each chapter and the page on which it begins. It is a guide for readers to find information. Look at the table of contents on the next page from a book about animals.

Table of Contents

Chapter 1   Mammals...3
Chapter 2   Birds...20
Chapter 3   Fish...32
Chapter 4   Reptiles 45
Chapter 5   Amphibians 55

If you wanted to find information about penguins, which page would you turn to? The table of contents shows that the chapter about birds begins on page 20.

An **index** is an important text feature, especially in nonfiction books. The index lists the topics that are covered and the page number (or numbers) on which the topic can be found in the book. An index appears in alphabetical (or ABC) order. Look at the index below from a science book.

eagle, 22, 27
eggs, 20, 32, 45, 55
elephants, 4, 14, 19

Where would you look if you wanted to find information about animal eggs?

Like text features, **graphic features** organize and explain information, but in a visual way. Graphic features include pictures, charts, some lists, graphs, time lines, diagrams, and maps that go along with the text. Graphic features show information and make it clearer.

Like all graphic features, a **chart** organizes information in a visual way. A chart may also show information not given in the text. Read the chart below.

President	Birth Date
George Washington	February 22, 1732
John Adams	October 30, 1735
Thomas Jefferson	April 13, 1743

Notice that the chart is organized in columns and rows. A chart makes it easier for readers to get information clearly and quickly.

Thinking It Through

Read the following index, and then answer the question that follows.

> **Alabama**, 17, 19–22
> **Alaska**, 18, 34–55
> **Arizona**, 10–32
> **Arkansas**, 37, 59, 76–77
> **California**, 22–40, 51, 60
> **Colorado**, 31, 34, 39–45
> **Connecticut**, 32, 41, 55–74, 87

How can you use the index to find information about Arkansas?

_____

_____

_____

_____

HINT Think about how topics are organized in an index. How would the index help you find the information you need?

Coached Example

Read the table of contents and answer the questions.

Chapter 1   Ships 12
Chapter 2   Trains...23
Chapter 3   Cars...39
Chapter 4   Airplanes 51
Chapter 5   Space Shuttles...72
Chapter 6   Inventors Long Ago.....................................90
Chapter 7   Inventors Today 103
Chapter 8   Inventing in the Future 115

1. In which chapter would you find information about sports cars?

   A. Chapter 1

   B. Chapter 3

   C. Chapter 5

   D. Chapter 7

   HINT The chapters are divided by topic. Think about which topic you are looking for.

2. In which chapter would you find information about the inventor of the lightbulb?

   A. Chapter 5

   B. Chapter 6

   C. Chapter 7

   D. Chapter 8

   HINT When was the lightbulb invented? The chapters separate inventors into different time periods.

Lesson Practice

Use the Reading Guide to help you understand the passage.

Reading Guide

How do the headings in bold print help you follow the passage?

If this passage appeared in a book, what words might you find in the index?

What facts does the list at the end of the passage give you about horses in the past that were not in the reading passage?

Horses in History

How Old Are Horses?

Horses have been on Earth even longer than humans. They have been here for about fifty million years! That's a long time. But it took millions of years for humans and horses to become friends.

Horses and Humans

During the Ice Ages in Europe, wild horses roamed the land. That was about forty thousand years ago. During that time, humans were settling that area. They were hunting horses and using them for food. They were also painting horses on cave walls. This showed that horses were part of ancient life.

Useful Animals

For more than five thousand years, horses have been living among people. Instead of hunting horses, humans used them for work, transportation, and other things. Humans gave horses food and a place to live.

Horses Today

Today, most people use cars, instead of horses, to get around. Farmers use tractors, not horses, to pull plows. But horses are still important to people. People use them for racing and for riding for fun. A horse is still a good friend.

Uses for Horses
transportation
moving heavy things
warfare
farming
companionship

Answer the following questions.

1. Under which heading in the passage would you find information about how long horses have been on Earth?

   A. How Old Are Horses?

   B. Horses and Humans

   C. Useful Animals

   D. Horses Today

2. What does the title tell you the passage will be about?

   A. It will be about what horses are like.

   B. It will be about horses throughout time.

   C. It will be about how humans use horses today.

   D. It will be about how humans will use horses in the future.

3. In which chapter from a table of contents would you MOST LIKELY find the passage about horses you have read?

   A. Animals in History

   B. Famous Battles in History

   C. Jobs in History

   D. Leaders in History

4. According to the list at the end of the passage, what were horses NOT used for?

   A. transportation

   B. helping soldiers in war

   C. getting rid of insects

   D. helping farmers

5. How does the list at the end of the passage help you better understand how humans used horses in the past?

   _____

   _____

   _____

   _____

   _____

Read the passage and answer the questions that follow.

Bird and Coyote

Long ago, Bluebird was Graybird. His wings and body matched the color of the dust. He blended in, and no one ever noticed him. Then one day, as he flew above a sparkling, sky-colored lake, he saw Butterfly. Her wings and body matched the bright blue of the lake exactly. Gasping, he landed nearby.

"Why are you staring at me?" asked the lovely Butterfly.

"You are so beautiful, as if you've been bathing in this lake. I wish more than anything I could be that color, too," said the honest bird.

Butterfly lowered her eyes and whispered, "You can be. Just follow what I tell you exactly."

Butterfly told Graybird to bathe in the lake four times daily for four days. With each bath, he had to face the four directions: North, South, East, and West. And most important, once he turned blue, he had to sing a special song thanking the lake for her help.

The eager bird did as Butterfly said. Soon, he was bluer than the sky. As he flew about, Bluebird sang songs about the wonderful lake.

This caught the attention of Coyote, who lived nearby.

"My goodness," said Coyote. "I've never seen feathers so blue. I wouldn't mind a little of that color for myself."

Bluebird told Coyote all about the lake and taught him how to change his rough coat from brown to blue.

"And remember to thank the lake for helping you," urged Bluebird.

Coyote couldn't wait. After four days, he, too, was blue. Sighing, Coyote stared at his reflection in the lake. "I am magnificent," he said. "I shall now be called Blue Coyote, and all animals will wish to look at me." Then Coyote strutted away to show off his coat.

Coyote became so boastful, he forgot to pay attention. He tripped, landing on his back in the mud. Jumping to his feet, he tried to brush off the mud—without luck. Coyote rolled in the dust, but his fur grew dustier and dustier. The beautiful blue color disappeared.

1. What is Graybird's problem in the passage?

   A. Graybird is afraid of Coyote.

   B. Graybird wants to change his color so that he can stand out.

   C. Graybird does not like his new color.

   D. Graybird forgets to follow Butterfly's instructions.

2. How is Coyote's problem really a problem within himself?

   A. Coyote is so forgetful that he doesn't remember Bluebird's instructions.

   B. Coyote is so selfish that he won't share the secret with any other animal.

   C. Coyote is so greedy that he wants to learn all of Butterfly's secrets.

   D. Coyote is so boastful that he doesn't pay attention and falls into the mud.

3. Read the last sentence from the passage.

   The beautiful blue color disappeared.

   Based on this sentence, what will Coyote MOST LIKELY do?

   A. He will make the blue color reappear.

   B. He will continue to roll in the dust.

   C. He will ask Bluebird for his help again.

   D. He will show off his rough, brown coat.

4. How do you know that the passage is an example of fiction?

   A. It uses real people to tell a story.

   B. It tells about events that could really happen.

   C. It uses animal characters and made-up events.

   D. It tells a true story.

Read the passage and answer the questions that follow.

The Story of My Life

excerpted and adapted from the autobiography of Helen Keller

My parents were sad and deeply troubled. We lived a long way from any school for the blind or the deaf. It seemed unlikely that anyone would come to such an out-of-the-way place as Tuscumbia, Alabama, to teach me—a child who was both deaf and blind. Indeed, my friends and relatives sometimes doubted whether I could be taught. My mother's only ray of hope came from Charles Dickens's "American Notes." She had read his account of Laura Bridgman, and remembered that she was deaf and blind. Yet she had been educated. But my mother also remembered that Dr. Skyline, who had discovered the way to teach the deaf and blind, had been dead many years. His methods had probably died with him. And if they had not, how was a little girl in a far-off town in Alabama going to receive the benefit of them?

When I was about six years old, my father heard of a good eye doctor in Baltimore, who had been successful in cases that had seemed hopeless. My parents took me to Baltimore to see if anything could be done for my eyes.

When we arrived in Baltimore, Dr. Chisholm received us kindly. Yet he could do nothing. He advised my father to consult Dr. Alexander Graham Bell of Washington, D.C. He said that Dr. Bell would be able to give Father information about schools and teachers of deaf or blind children. We went immediately to Washington, D.C., to see Dr. Bell. At the time, I was totally unaware of my father's doubts that Dr. Bell would be able to help me. All I could feel was the excitement of moving from place to place. Child as I was, I at once felt the tenderness and sympathy which endeared Dr. Bell to so many people, as his achievements gained their admiration. He held me on his knee while I examined his watch, and he made it strike for me. He understood the signs I made, and I knew it and loved him at once. But I did not dream that that interview would be the door through which I should pass from darkness into light, from isolation to friendship, knowledge, and love.

Dr. Bell advised my father to write to Mr. Anagnos, director of the Perkins Institution, where Dr. Skyline had done his great work with the blind. Father was to ask Mr. Anagnos if he knew a good teacher for me. This my father did. In a few weeks there came a letter from Mr. Anagnos with the great news that a teacher had been found. This was in the summer of 1886. But Miss Sullivan did not arrive until the following March.

5. Which is the BEST question to ask yourself as you read the passage?

   A. How large is Alabama?

   B. How large is Baltimore?

   C. What is it like for a deaf or blind person to go to school?

   D. What does Dr. Chisholm look like?

6. Why did the author write this passage?

   A. to persuade readers to agree with her

   B. to tell the true story of her life

   C. to tell how to make something

   D. to entertain people with a story about a teacher

7. What is the main idea of the passage?

   A. Helen Keller and her family struggled to find a good school or teacher for her.

   B. Helen Keller and her family found good teachers close to home.

   C. Students have been going to school for more than a hundred years.

   D. Alexander Graham Bell was Helen Keller's teacher.

8. What conclusion can you draw from reading the passage?

   A. It is fun to move from place to place.

   B. It is hard for anyone to find a teacher.

   C. Baltimore is a nice city.

   D. It is not easy to teach a student who is deaf and blind.

Read the passage and answer the questions that follow.

Alexander Graham Bell

Early Life

Alexander Graham Bell was born in Scotland on March 3, 1847. His mother educated him at home. Although his mother was nearly deaf, she was skilled at playing the piano. Bell's father studied speech and language. He tried to improve communication for deaf people. Bell was also expected to study speech and language and help the deaf.

Young Man in North America

At age 23, Bell and his parents moved to North America. They settled in Canada. His father continued to give speeches about new ways for people who could not hear to understand speech.

Soon, Alexander Graham Bell moved to Boston. He worked in a school for deaf children and tutored deaf students. One of his deaf students was Mabel Hubbard. One day, Bell was playing the piano and singing at the Hubbard home. He noticed that his voice carried along the strings of the piano keys. At that moment, he realized that voices could be carried through wires.

Meeting the Hubbard family changed Bell's life. Bell fell in love with Mabel. Her father supported him in his dream to build the first telephone.

Race for the Telephone

Bell did many experiments with the telephone. But another inventor, Elisha Gray, was also trying to invent the telephone. Mr. Hubbard knew that Bell had to hurry to complete his telephone before Gray invented it first. So, Hubbard gave Bell a helper. His name was Thomas Watson.

Mr. Hubbard heard that Gray was going to apply for a patent for his telephone. He was worried that Gray would get the rights to make the telephone before Bell. On February 14, 1876, Bell applied for his patent. Hours later, so did Gray. The race was on!

On March 7, 1876, Bell received his patent. Three days later, he tested his telephone. The telephone worked!

Later Life

After the success of the telephone, Bell returned to teaching the deaf. Years later, Bell went back to inventing. His inventions changed the way people lived.

9. Which is the BEST question to ask yourself as you are reading the passage?

   A. What happened to Bell's mother and father?

   B. How did the work of Alexander Graham Bell change people's lives?

   C. How many people in the world have patents?

   D. What else happened on March 7, 1876?

10. How is this passage different from a fiction passage?

   A. It has imaginary characters, a setting, and a plot.

   B. It uses facts to tell about real people and events.

   C. It uses *I* to tell a story.

   D. It tells about someone's childhood.

11. What is the main idea of the passage?

   A. Alexander Graham Bell taught a deaf student named Mabel Hubbard.

   B. Alexander Graham Bell's father studied speech and language.

   C. Alexander Graham Bell invented things that changed the way people lived.

   D. Alexander Graham Bell moved to Boston, Massachusetts.

12. Which heading in bold (dark) print from the passage tells about Alexander Graham Bell's childhood?

   A. Early Life

   B. Young Man in North America

   C. Race for the Telephone

   D. Later Life

13. Which detail supports the main idea that Bell's inventions changed the way people lived?

    A. He invented the telephone.

    B. He helped the deaf.

    C. He started a school for deaf children.

    D. He noticed that voices could be carried through wires.

14. What conclusion can you draw about Alexander Graham Bell?

    A. He was deaf.

    B. He was a great teacher and inventor.

    C. He did not care about people with problems.

    D. He was determined to become a full-time inventor.

15. How is Helen Keller's autobiography like the biography of Alexander Graham Bell? How is it different?

_____

_____

_____

_____

16. If the passage about Bell appeared in a book about famous inventors, what kind of text features might you find? How would these text features help you better understand the passage?

_____

_____

_____

_____

CHAPTER

3 Writing

Lesson 17 Author's Purpose and Audience
3.9.a

Lesson 18 Prewriting Strategies
3.9.b, 3.9.e

Lesson 19 Topic Sentences and Paragraphs
3.9.c, 3.9.d, 3.9.f

Lesson 20 Revising Writing
3.9.g

Lesson 21 Writing a Short Report
3.7.a, 3.11.a–d, 3.12

Chapter 3 Review

17 Author's Purpose and Audience

3.9.a

Getting the Idea

Author's Purpose

The **author's purpose** is the reason an author writes something. Usually, an author's purpose for writing is to entertain readers, to inform or explain, or to persuade.

Entertain

Writing that **entertains** lets readers have fun. This type of writing is usually fiction. It may be a poem, a play, or a story with made-up characters, a setting, and a plot. Read the example below.

> Fido was one of the funniest dogs in the neighborhood. The other dogs would listen to him tell jokes in the backyard late at night. The other dogs would howl in response. Every dog loved Fido's jokes.

This example could not take place in real life. You know it is fiction because of the animal characters and imaginary events. The author wrote the story to entertain the readers, or audience.

Inform

Writing that **informs** uses facts and explains ideas to an audience. This writing gives information to a reader. It is usually nonfiction writing. Textbooks, essays, newspaper and magazine articles, and science and history books are all examples of nonfiction. Read the example below.

> The United States is in North America. To the north of the United States is the country of Canada. To the south is the country of Mexico. These countries make up the continent of North America.

Persuade

Writing that **persuades** tries to get readers to think or act in a certain way. If a writer's purpose is to persuade, the writer tries to get the audience to agree with his or her **opinion**. You encounter this purpose for writing every day. Advertisements and commercials are examples of persuasive writing. Their purpose is to get you to buy, think, or do something. Clue words such as *should*, *need*, *ought to*, *I think*, *I believe*, or *in my opinion* are hints that the writer is trying to persuade the reader, or audience. Read the example below.

> We cannot let the library close without a fight! We all use the library, so in my opinion, we should all work hard to keep it open. Join me at a fund-raiser this Saturday to raise money to save the library!

The writer is trying to persuade the audience to join him in saving the library.

Authors may have other purposes for writing. Sometimes an author's purpose is to explain how to do or make something. Cookbooks, how-to books, and user manuals have the purpose of explaining something, step-by-step, so that it is easy for the reader to follow.

Another purpose for writing is to describe. A poet's purpose might be to describe something beautiful in a poem. When an author's purpose is to describe, he or she writes in a way that lets the audience see, hear, smell, taste, or feel something in the same way that the writer does.

Audience

Before an author decides on a purpose for writing, he or she must think about the audience. The **audience** is the reader. Authors need to ask themselves these questions before they write.

- Who will I be writing for?
- How much does my audience already know about my topic?

For example, readers of stories want to be entertained. The audience for a new science or history book might want to learn some new information.

When you know your audience, you will be able to get a clearer purpose for your writing.

Thinking It Through

Read the following paragraph, and then answer the questions that follow.

At many libraries, the magazine rack has every type of magazine. Recently, more computer magazines have filled the rack than any other type of magazine. Computer magazines have now replaced some news and hobby magazines. For the general reader, however, there are still plenty of sports and Hollywood gossip magazines on the rack.

What is the author's purpose for writing this paragraph? How do you know?

_____

_____

_____

_____

HINT   Think about who the audience is for this paragraph and what the author is trying to tell the reader.

Coached Example

Read the passage and answer the questions.

Dear Mrs. Lewis,

Thank you for speaking to our class today. We are glad that you care about making the playground safer. We hope that you can do many of the things you talked to us about. We need handlebars on the ladder going up to the slide. That would keep many students from falling on the stairs. We need to have the branches trimmed from trees so that they do not fall on us.

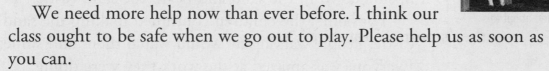

We need more help now than ever before. I think our class ought to be safe when we go out to play. Please help us as soon as you can.

Thank you,
Tricia West

1. What is the author's purpose in writing the passage?

   A. to entertain

   B. to persuade

   C. to explain

   D. to inform

   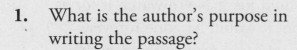 Look for clue words that suggest the author's purpose.

2. Who is the audience for the passage?

   A. students in Tricia West's class

   B. Tricia West

   C. Mrs. Lewis, a woman at Tricia's school

   D. Tricia West's teacher

   HINT The passage is a letter. Read the letter to figure out who the audience for the letter will be.

Lesson Practice

Use the Reading Guide to help you understand the passage.

Reading Guide

What kind of passage is this? Does it have characters, a setting, and a plot?

Who do you think the author wrote this passage for?

How do you think the audience felt about this passage?

Sand Castles

Gina and Jack set out early in the morning to make their sand castle. They went to the beach with three pails and two shovels. They knew they could use seashells to decorate their finished castle.

Gina ran to the water, filled her pail with sand, and added some water. She was the first to place the pail upside down in the sand and begin the sand castle.

For hours, the children continued making the sand castle. People walking by would watch them and smile. Everyone was amazed at the work they were doing.

Finally, when they were finished, Gina and Jack sat back and admired their work. Suddenly, Jack noticed something. The tide was coming in fast. It would wash away their castle within an hour or so.

Jack knew there was nothing they could do to save the sand castle. They would just have to watch it for as long as they could. Soon, it would be gone forever.

Just then, their dad appeared next to them with a camera. "Don't worry about the sand castle," he said. "I can take your picture with it, and then we'll have the sand castle forever."

Dad had them pose for the photo. That picture stayed in their living room for many years.

Answer the following questions.

1. What is the author's purpose for writing the passage?

   A. to entertain

   B. to inform

   C. to explain

   D. to persuade

2. Which clues helped you answer question 1?

   A. The author gives many opinions.

   B. The author lists steps in order.

   C. The author includes a story with characters, a setting, and a plot.

   D. The author gives many facts.

3. Who is MOST LIKELY the audience for the passage?

   A. college students

   B. adults learning to build sand castles

   C. people who want to give money to clean the beaches

   D. children reading a story for fun

4. This passage would MOST LIKELY be in a

   A. cookbook.

   B. book about beaches.

   C. newspaper.

   D. book of stories.

5. What is another purpose an author could have for writing about sand castles?

   _____

   _____

   _____

   _____

18 Prewriting Strategies

3.9.b, 3.9.e

Getting the Idea

You probably use prewriting strategies to find an idea or a topic for your writing. **Prewriting** is the first step before you begin to write. Prewriting may include brainstorming with other students to get ideas for your writing. Once you have an idea, you might use another prewriting strategy. You might make a list or a chart of ideas, for example. Prewriting helps you plan and organize your ideas before you begin to write.

Suppose you wanted to write a story. Once you had an idea, you would use narrative writing. **Narrative writing** tells a story. When you plan a story, you need to think about the **characters**, **setting**, and **plot**. You also need to think about the narrator. The **narrator** is the person who tells the story.

Before you write a story, ask yourself, What is my narrator's point of view? The **point of view** is the viewpoint from which the narrator tells the story. You will also need to decide on the problem in the story. The **problem** is the conflict in the plot. Ask yourself what the **solution** to the problem will be. Then use a sequence chart to plan the order of events in the plot. A **sequence chart** is a graphic organizer. A **graphic organizer** will help you plan and organize your ideas before you begin to write.

Look at the sequence chart below. It shows the events in a story about Joe.

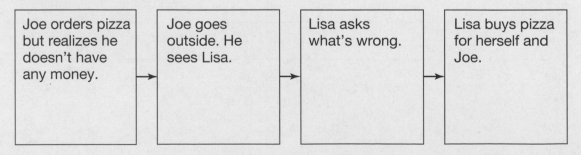

The sequence chart shows the order of events in the story. The first box introduces the problem, or conflict, in the plot. The middle boxes show how the plot develops. Often, the middle of the story has description and **dialogue**. The last box shows how the problem is solved at the end of the story.

Now suppose you wanted to write a nonfiction article for your school magazine. Once you had an idea for your article, you would use informational writing. **Informational writing** gives facts and information about a topic. It also explains ideas. Its purpose is to **inform**. Another name for this type of writing is **expository writing**. Once you have an idea, plan how to organize your writing. For example, if you want to **compare and contrast** two animals in your article, you could use a Venn diagram. A **Venn diagram** shows how two things are alike and how they are different. Look at the Venn diagram below.

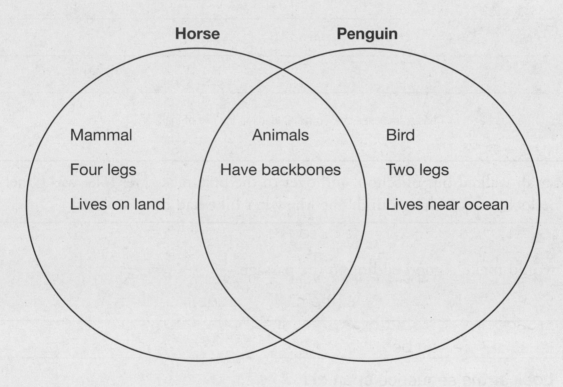

Horse   **Penguin**

Mammal   Animals   Bird

Four legs   Have backbones   Two legs

Lives on land   Lives near ocean

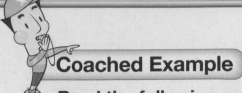

Coached Example

Read the following passages. Then answer the questions.

1. Al's cat was playing outside when the neighbor's dog began barking. Dogs like barking at squirrels and joggers. Suddenly, the cat ran up a tree. Al climbed the tree to bring his cat down.

Which sentence does NOT move the plot along?

_____

_____

_____

_____

HINT Remember, a plot has a sequence of events that leads to the end of the story.

2. Mariah walked out of school and over to the bike rack. Her bike was gone! The lock was on the ground. She knew her bike had been stolen.

What would make a good ending to the passage?

_____

_____

_____

_____

HINT Read the passage again. How could the problem be solved at the end?

Lesson Practice

Use the Writing Guide to help you understand the passage.

Writing Guide

Who are the characters?

What is the setting?

How does the dialogue develop the plot?

Danny's Birthday Treat

On Friday afternoon, Danny asked his grandmother what she would like for her birthday. She asked him to make something for her. "Make something?" Danny thought. "What can I make?" That night he asked his dad to help him think of something to make.

"Well," Dad said, "I know she likes to have a sweet treat now and then. Why don't you make her a birthday cake?"

Mom was listening. "Cakes are pretty hard if you've never made one. How about banana bread? It's a tasty treat, and it's easy to make. I'll help you if you need me."

The next day Mom and Danny looked up a recipe for banana bread. Then they went to the store and bought all the ingredients. When they got home, Danny followed the steps in the recipe. He started by mixing the dry ingredients together. Mom didn't need to help until it was time to pour the batter into the pan. Then she put the pan in the oven. That night Danny gave Gran her present. She loved every bite!

What is the problem? How is it solved?

_____

_____

_____

_____

_____

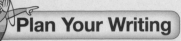

Plan Your Writing

Read the writing prompt, and then plan your response below.

Write a story about a girl or a boy who is on vacation when something surprising happens. Tell how this surprising event causes a problem. Describe the problem and tell how it is solved at the end of the story. Be sure to give the events in the story in the order that they happened. Use description, dialogue, and a solid conclusion.

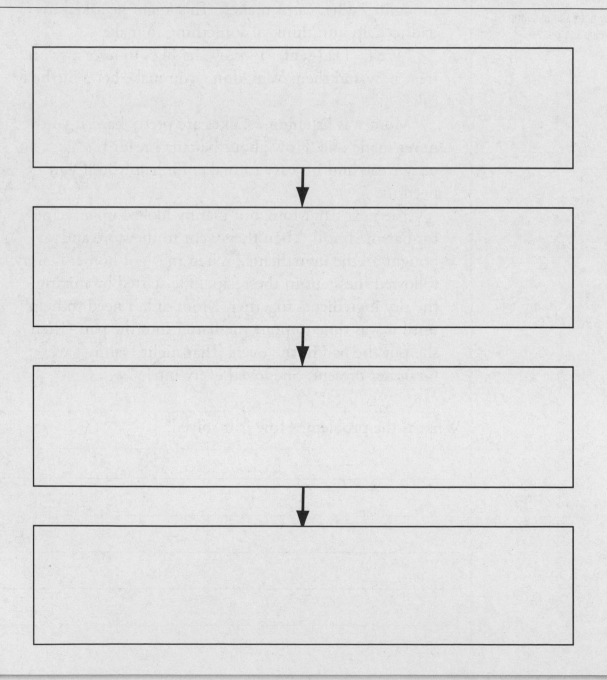

Write Your Response

Write your response in the space provided. You may use your own paper if you need more space.

_____

_____

_____

_____

_____

_____

_____

_____

_____

_____

_____

_____

_____

_____

_____

_____

_____

_____

19 Topic Sentences and Paragraphs

3.9.c, 3.9.d, 3.9.f

Getting the Idea

Good writing begins with a clear topic sentence. A **topic sentence** states the **main idea** of a paragraph or a passage. Often, the topic sentence is the first sentence. It sets up the supporting details and sentences that follow the main idea. A paragraph that gives information about space travel might begin with the underlined topic sentence below.

<u>Traveling to the moon is not difficult, but traveling to the stars would be.</u> **First**, our spaceships travel at limited speeds. It might take 80,000 years to get to the nearest star. **Next**, astronauts would die long before the trip was over. **Then**, there is a speed limit in space. This is the speed of light. Since nothing can go faster than the speed of light, our spaceships could not reach the stars any quicker. **Finally**, until scientists find a way to solve the problem of traveling faster than the speed of light, there will be no "star treks" in the near future.

Look at the underlined topic sentence. It states the main idea of the paragraph—the problems with traveling to the stars. The supporting sentences give details about the main idea and show each of the problems.

Look at how the example paragraph is organized. It uses transition words to present each of the problems. **Transition words** help readers connect ideas. Read the transition words in bold (dark) print in the paragraph. The words *first*, *next*, *then*, and *finally* show time order in the paragraph. They also help to organize the writing.

There are many ways to organize your writing. Some writing will compare and contrast people, things, or ideas. Other writing will include information in the order that events happen. However you organize your writing, your paragraph should begin with a clear topic sentence. It should end with a strong closing sentence, or conclusion. A **conclusion** restates or sums up the main idea of your writing. It is usually the last sentence. In the example paragraph, the conclusion begins with the transition word *finally*. This word signals that the paragraph is coming to an end.

A **graphic organizer** is a good way to organize your ideas for writing. Suppose you wanted to write an informational paragraph about the famous American nurse Clara Barton. You could use a web to organize your ideas. A **web** is a graphic organizer that has the topic or topic sentence in the center. It has ideas and supporting details about the topic in the ovals around it. Think about your topic sentence first. Then think about the ideas that will support it. Look at the web below.

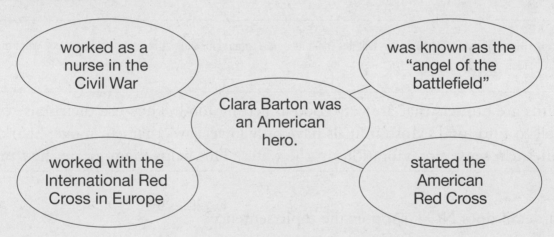

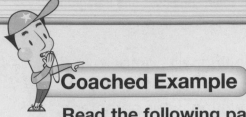

Coached Example

Read the following paragraphs. Then answer the questions.

1. Amelia Earhart liked airplanes. She was the first woman to cross the Atlantic Ocean by airplane and the first woman to make a solo flight across the Atlantic. Amelia Earhart was the first person to fly alone from Honolulu to California.

How can you write the first sentence to make the main idea of the paragraph clearer?

_____

_____

_____

HINT Remember, a topic sentence tells the main idea of a paragraph. Look at the supporting details. What main idea do they support?

2. Sharks are hunters that are very good at getting food. They use their sense of smell to find food. Most animals have only lower jaws that can move. Sharks' bodies can sense tiny vibrations in the water. This helps them locate their prey.

Which detail does NOT support the topic sentence?

_____

_____

_____

HINT Read the paragraph again. What is the main idea? Which sentence does not support the main idea and does not belong in the paragraph?

Lesson Practice

Use the Writing Guide to help you understand the passage.

Writing Guide

What is the topic sentence? How does it state the main idea of the passage?

Look at paragraph 2. What are the transition words in the paragraph?

How does the closing sentence summarize the main idea?

A Remarkable Man

Ben Franklin was a man who achieved many great things. He was an inventor, a printer, and a writer. He was also a founder of our country. Franklin was born in Boston, Massachusetts, on January 17, 1706. Believe it or not, he attended school for only two years! Why? His family was poor, and he needed to work. There were a lot of poor people in the country.

At age 12, Franklin started working in his brother's printing shop. However, when the two brothers didn't get along, Franklin left by the age of 16. First, he went to New York. Next, he settled in Philadelphia, Pennsylvania. Then, he opened his own printing shop there. He started a newspaper and wrote an almanac.

Ben Franklin loved Philadelphia and worked hard to make it a good place for people to live. He set up the first fire department, hospital, and library. Libraries are good places to find books. He also invented many things. His inventions included the lightning rod, the Franklin stove, and a type of eyeglasses. Later, Franklin helped write the Declaration of Independence and the Constitution. Ben Franklin died on April 17, 1790, at the age of 84. He was truly a remarkable man!

Which sentences are off the topic?

_____

_____

_____

_____

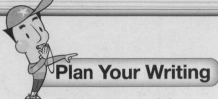

Plan Your Writing

Read the writing prompt, and then plan your response below.

Think about an important event in American history. Write a paragraph that tells about the event. When and where did the event take place? Who was involved? Why did the event happen? How did it end? Be sure to include the main idea in your topic sentence. Use important details to support the main idea.

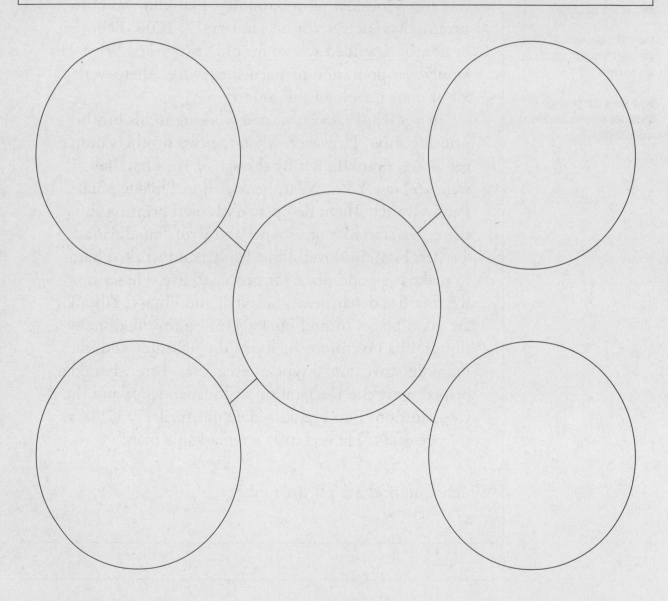

Write Your Response

Write your response in the space provided. You may use your own paper if you need more space.

_____

_____

_____

_____

_____

_____

_____

_____

_____

_____

_____

_____

_____

_____

_____

_____

_____

_____

_____

20 Revising Writing

3.9.g

Getting the Idea

A writer does not usually hand in his or her first try at writing. A **draft** is one of the first versions of a writer's work. A writer may make more than one draft before he or she hands in a final draft.

A writer can revise a draft to make it better. When you **revise** a draft, you make changes and corrections to it. Sometimes a teacher gives good advice about how to revise your writing. You may also ask a classmate or friend to read your draft and make suggestions.

When you revise your draft, look at the organization and the details of your writing. The paragraphs below will help you revise.

Organization

Each paragraph should have a topic sentence, or main idea. All of the details in that paragraph should be about the topic sentence. Look for transition words and ideas in an order that makes sense. There should be clear connections between ideas in the same paragraph. Get rid of any ideas that do not belong. Make sure your sentences are in the right order.

Details

Check for good, clear **supporting details** that back up, the main idea. Add the details that will best help your reader understand your topic sentence. These details may be facts, examples, and descriptions.

When you **edit** your draft, fix mistakes in grammar, spelling, capitalization, and punctuation. Make sure your sentences are written clearly and correctly. Check your final draft against your earlier drafts. Make sure you have corrected all your mistakes. Be sure to include all the necessary changes. Pay special attention to spacing between words, sentences, and paragraphs.

Read this example of a student's draft.

> To make a tambourine, you will need two strong paper plates, a stapler or glue, a hole punch, string, small jingle bells, and markers. First, staple or glue the paper plates together facing each other. ~~Staplers were first invented in the 1800's.~~ Finally, decorate your tambourine. Next, use the hole punch to make holes around the edges. Then, use the string to tie a jingle bell to each hole. String can also be used for lots of other uses. It's time to make some music!

The first thing you might notice is the sentence that is crossed out. Some sentences do not add anything to a paragraph. They are not needed and should be removed. Do you see any other sentences that need to be removed?

Are the sentences in the correct order? Look at the transition words in the paragraph. They are *first*, *next*, *then*, and *finally*. The sentence "Finally, decorate your tambourine" should be placed before the last sentence in the paragraph. Make sure to spend the time revising and editing your draft. Then make a neat, final copy.

You can use a computer to type your final draft. When your final draft is ready, you can publish it. To **publish** means to let others read your work. For example, you can print out your final draft and let others read it. You can e-mail it or post it online. Be sure to let others enjoy your writing.

Thinking It Through

Read the following paragraph, and then answer the questions that follow.

Richard is a firefighter. Last week he ran into a burning building and rescued three young children. Then, he put out the fire. Later, Richard went home and ate dinner. Richard loves being a firefighter.

Which detail does NOT belong in the paragraph? Why?

_____

_____

_____

_____

HINT Read the paragraph again. Look for the detail that has nothing to do with the rest of the paragraph.

Coached Example

Read the passage and answer the questions.

School was cancelled because of a big snowstorm. Jeremy thought, "I can earn some extra money by shoveling driveways." After breakfast, Jeremy got the shovel and knocked on his neighbor's door. Jeremy ate a bowl of oatmeal and thought of which neighbors to ask. Mr. Hernandez told Jeremy he could shovel the sidewalk and the driveway. Mr. Hernandez and his family came from Mexico. After Jeremy finished shoveling, Mr. Hernandez paid Jeremy ten dollars.

1. Which sentence is in the wrong order in the passage?

    A. "Jeremy ate a bowl of oatmeal and thought of which neighbors to ask."

    B. "After breakfast, Jeremy got the shovel and knocked on his neighbor's door."

    C. "Mr. Hernandez told Jeremy he could shovel the sidewalk and the driveway."

    D. "After Jeremy finished shoveling, Mr. Hernandez paid Jeremy ten dollars."

    HINT First, Jeremy needs to eat breakfast. Then, he can get started shoveling snow.

2. Which sentence does NOT belong in this passage?

    A. "Jeremy ate a bowl of oatmeal and thought of which neighbors to ask."

    B. "Mr. Hernandez told Jeremy he could shovel the sidewalk and the driveway."

    C. "Mr. Hernandez and his family came from Mexico."

    D. "After Jeremy finished shoveling, Mr. Hernandez paid Jeremy ten dollars."

    HINT Remember, details not related to the passage need to be taken out.

Lesson Practice

Use the Reading Guide to help you understand the passage.

Reading Guide

Are the sentences in the correct order?

Which details are not related to the passage?

Are there any details that could be added?

Special Effects in Movies

If you have seen a movie lately, chances are you have seen or heard special effects. Special effects have been around since the beginning of movies. A special effect is anything that is unreal that makes the viewer think that it is real. Some of the earliest special effects were makeup and costumes. People wear costumes on Halloween. Special effects could be used to make an actor look like an animal, an alien, or even a monster.

Models were another kind of early special effect. When model spaceships were hung from strings, they looked as if they were floating or flying. You might see a space battle with tiny model spaceships. In some older movies, you might even see some of the strings used to move the models. Most of the time, these tricks fooled the audience.

Today, special effects rely heavily on computers. You might see real actors interact with imaginary characters. Today's movie monsters and aliens have come a long way since the early days of special effects. Computers can also be used to play video games.

Answer the following questions.

1. Which sentence does NOT belong in paragraph 1?

   A. "Special effects have been around since the beginning of movies."

   B. "Some of the earliest special effects were makeup and costumes."

   C. "People wear costumes on Halloween."

   D. "Special effects could be used to make an actor look like an animal, an alien, or even a monster."

2. Which would be the BEST detail to add to paragraph 1?

   A. how costumes were made

   B. the different kinds of monsters

   C. the types of animals

   D. the color of the makeup

3. Which would be the BEST detail to add to paragraph 2?

   A. the other kinds of models used

   B. what type of string was used

   C. why there was a space battle

   D. the names of the space battles

4. Which sentence does NOT belong in paragraph 3?

   A. "Today, special effects rely heavily on computers."

   B. "Computers can also be used to play video games."

   C. "You might see real actors interact with imaginary characters."

   D. "Today's movie monsters and aliens have come a long way since the early days of special effects."

5. Which sentences are in the wrong order in paragraph 2? Where would you move them?

   _____

   _____

   _____

   _____

21 Writing a Short Report

3.7.a, 3.11.a–d, 3.12

Getting the Idea

There are many different kinds of writing. Sometimes, you will be asked to explain something or to give information about a famous person or an event. For this kind of writing, you will need to do research. When you do **research**, you get facts and information from resources such as books, encyclopedias, newspapers, and Web sites.

A **resource** is any material that helps a writer find information. When you write a research report, it is important to use resources you can trust. A **research report** deals with a topic that is based on trustworthy information from resources. There are many resources in a library. There are books, encyclopedias, magazines, newspapers, journals, and DVDs. There are also computers. A computer can help you research Web sites and use DVDs. Computers are very helpful for finding information. As you read the resources, take notes.

When you do research, you need to give an author credit if you are using his or her words exactly. Keep track of all the resources you use in your writing. A **bibliography** is a list of the resources you have used for a research report or paper. Look at the next page for some sample entries from a bibliography for a research report about ice-skating.

A Book by a Single Author
Vega, Sandra. Ice-Skating. Chicago: Sports Press, 2009.
   (Author)   (Title of work) (City)   (Publisher) (Year)

A Book by More Than One Author
Bock, Jan and Kim Chen. The Winter Olympics. Boston: Blue Books, 2003.
      (Authors)   (Title of Work)   (City)   (Publisher) (Year)

A Magazine Article
Hu, Liz. "Best Places to Ice-Skate." Skating Monthly. July 2010: 45–48.
(Author)   (Title of Article)   (Title of Magazine)   (Date) (Pages)

The final step before you write is to organize your notes. There are different ways to organize them. One way is by making an outline. An **outline** is a list of ideas in the order that you plan to write about them. An outline will help you keep track of main ideas and facts you have gathered. An outline for a research report about ice-skating can look like this:

Topic: Ice-Skating
I. History of Ice-Skating
    A. When did people first begin to ice-skate?
    B. How was ice-skating then different from ice-skating today?
II. Ice-Skating Today
    A. Where do people skate?
    B. What equipment do they need?
III. Ice-Skating as a Career
    A. What are the Olympics?
    B. What is the history of ice-skating in the Olympics?
    C. How do people skate as a career?

Notice that the topic of the research report is written at the top of the outline. Each Roman numeral (I, II, III) gives a main idea. Each capital letter (A, B, C) gives a question. Each question will be answered with details that support the main idea.

Thinking It Through

Read the following entries from a bibliography, and then answer the questions that follow.

Little, Clyde and Omar Smith. <u>Brown Bears</u>. New York: Big Planet Press, 2007.

McGuire, Seamus. <u>Brown Bears in California</u>. San Francisco: Wild California Publishing, 2002.

Wolff, Catherine. "The Disappearing Bear." <u>Nature Lover Monthly</u>. February 2008: 145–158.

Based on the bibliography, what is the topic of the research report?

_____

_____

_____

_____

_____

HINT Read the entries again. What do they have in common?

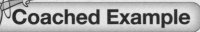

Coached Example

Read the passage and answer the questions.

Our class went to the library today. We have to write a research report about any topic we want. I am going to write mine about bicycling. There were a few books and magazine articles about the topic. I also looked at Web sites on the computer. Here's what my bibliography looks like so far:

Shearsman, Augusto. <u>Bicycles Through Time</u>. Brooklyn: Peloton Publishing, 2007.

Topovsky, Boris. "Cycling in the Past." <u>Bicycle Weekly</u>. 1 January 2010: 77, 131–138.

Tremaine, Laura. <u>The History of Cycling</u>. Portland: Tabor Press, 2006.

---

1. Which resources did the author NOT look at in the library?

   A. books

   B. Web sites

   C. DVDs

   D. magazine articles

   HINT Read the passage and the bibliography again. Which resource was not mentioned in the passage?

2. What does the bibliography include?

   A. a list of writers who like bicycling more than other sports

   B. a list of Web sites about bicycling

   C. a list of resources the writer will use to write a research report

   D. a list of resources the writer would like to read for fun

   HINT Think about what a bibliography is used for.

Plan Your Writing

Read the writing prompt, and then plan your response below.

Choose a famous person from history. Perhaps the person was an explorer or one of our presidents. Research the person's life. Use resources from the library or go to a Web site for information. Take notes on what you find out. Use a flowchart to organize the important events in the person's life. Tell about the events in the order that they happened. List your resources in your bibliography. Then write your report on the next page.

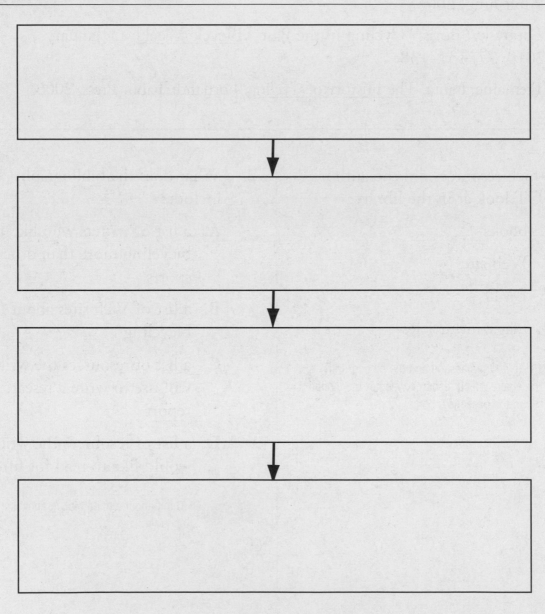

Write Your Response

Write your response in the space provided. You may use your own paper if you need more space.

_____

_____

_____

_____

_____

_____

_____

_____

_____

_____

_____

_____

_____

_____

_____

_____

_____

_____

_____

_____

_____

CHAPTER

3 Review

This passage contains mistakes. Read the passage and answer the questions that follow.

Teamwork

(1) Sometimes a basketball game can teach you a good lesson about teamwork. (2) Just ask Lani and Ginny. (3) Ginny was on the Sharks basketball team. (4) Some sharks are very dangerous. (5) At school she said to Lani, "We're going to win that game. (6) Your team doesn't have a chance." (7) Though she said this with a smile, her words stung Lani.

(8) Lani's team, the Wolves, were going to play against the Sharks. (9) Some of the girls in Lani's class played for the Sharks. (10) Of course, they were hoping that the Sharks would win. (11) Lani bought a new pair of sneakers before the game.

(12) Lani was excited about the upcoming basketball game. (13) Her team had won all their games this season. (14) But the Wolves were going to play one more game. (15) If they won, they would be the league champions.

(16) "No, the Wolves are going to win," said Lani.

(17) The day of the big game came at last. (18) The Wolves played well. (19) Lani scored two baskets. (20) In the end, the Sharks won, 35–34.

(21) After the game, Lani tried to be a good loser. (22) She even told the Sharks they had played a good game.

(23) When Monday came, Lani didn't want to go to school. (24) She told her mom, "They will surely tease me about losing the game."

(25) Lani walked slowly into her classroom. (26) She didn't see Ginny smiling. (27) Ginny and Lani were in the same group. (28) The first thing the teacher did was to divide the class into groups to do a project.

(29) "Oh, no," thought Lani. (30) "Now I will have to hear all about how much better Ginny's team is than my team."

(31) However, Ginny did not even mention the game as they worked together.

(32) At lunch, Ginny sat beside Lani. (33) Ginny smiled and didn't say a word. (34) Ginny's mom makes really good tuna sandwiches. (35) Lani said, "Thanks for not talking about the basketball game."

(36) Ginny said, "Well, I was happy we won. (37) But the game is over." (38) Ginny added, "Today, you and I are on the same team!"

1. What is the author's purpose for writing the passage?

   A. to entertain

   B. to inform

   C. to describe

   D. to persuade

2. Who is the audience for the passage?

   A. students doing research for a report

   B. people who want to enjoy reading a story

   C. people who want to learn to play basketball

   D. people who coach basketball teams

3. Read sentence 1 from the passage.

   Sometimes a basketball game can teach you a good lesson about teamwork.

   Why is this sentence the topic sentence of the passage?

   A. It shows that sports are just as important as all the other school subjects.

   B. It states the idea that winners are sometimes losers.

   C. It tells the main idea of the passage—that winning is everything.

   D. It tells the main idea of the passage—that teamwork is more than just playing a game.

4. How could the author have organized the events before writing the story?

   A. by making a word web

   B. by making a Venn diagram

   C. by using transition words

   D. by making a sequence chart

5. Which clues in the passage give you a hint about the author's purpose?

   A. The author explains how to do something.

   B. The author tries to get the reader to think in a certain way.

   C. The author gives facts and explains a topic.

   D. The author uses characters, a setting, and a plot to tell a story.

6. What age group would make a good audience for this passage?

   A. an audience that is a lot younger than the characters

   B. an audience that is a lot older than the characters

   C. an audience that is about the same age as the characters

   D. an audience that is Lani's mother's age

7. Which sentence from paragraph 1 does NOT support the topic and needs to be taken out or revised?

   A. sentence 3

   B. sentence 4

   C. sentence 6

   D. sentence 7

8. Read the last sentence from the passage.

   Ginny added, "Today, you and I are on the same team!"

   How does this sentence support the main idea?

   A. It offers a supporting detail.

   B. It summarizes the main idea of the passage.

   C. It brings the passage to a silly end.

   D. It does not repeat the topic sentence.

Informational Prompt

Virginia is home to the beautiful Blue Ridge Mountains. Write a short research report about the Blue Ridge Mountains. You might focus on its name, its history, or on its plants or animals. Use resources from the library or go to a Web site. Take notes on what you find out. Organize your ideas in a chart or another graphic organizer. List your resources in your bibliography. Then write your report on the next page. Use the checklist below to do your best writing.

Does your research report

❑ have a clear and focused topic?

❑ have a logical structure?

❑ present information clearly?

❑ use transitional words and phrases to connect ideas?

❑ use a style and vocabulary that is correct for the purpose and audience?

❑ have a solid conclusion?

❑ have good spelling, capitalization, and punctuation?

❑ follow the rules for good grammar?

Write your response on the page provided. You may use your own paper if you need more space.

CHAPTER

4 Editing and Grammar

Lesson 22 Spelling
3.10.j

Lesson 23 Articles and
Abbreviations
3.10.g, 3.10.i

Lesson 24 Possessives and
Contractions
3.10.e, 3.10.h

Lesson 25 Verb Tenses
3.10.d

Lesson 26 Sentence Structure
3.10.a–c, 3.10.f

Chapter 4 Review

22 Spelling

3.10.j

Getting the Idea

Spelling is the correct way of ordering letters in words. When you write, it is important to spell each word correctly. This will help your writing to be clear. When your writing is clear, your reader will be able to follow your ideas. Look at the spelling rules below.

Spelling Rule	Example
Put *i* before *e*, except after *c*, or when the word sounds like *neighbor* or *weigh*.	ch**ie**f, bel**ie**ve, f**ie**ld, n**ie**ce **cei**ling, re**cei**ve, **ei**ght, sl**ei**gh
If a word ends in silent *e*, drop the *e* before adding *-ed* or *-ing*.	bak**e** + **-ed** = bak**ed** hop**e** + **-ing** = hop**ing**
If a one-syllable word ends with one vowel and one consonant, double the consonant before adding *-ed or -ing.*	h**ug** + **-ed** = hu**gged** ch**op** + **-ing** = cho**pping**
The final long *e* sound in a two-syllable word is often spelled *y* or *ey.*	read**y**, sorr**y**, beaut**y** turk**ey**, hock**ey**, journ**ey**
For a verb that ends with a consonant + *y,* change *y* to *i* and add *-es* or *-ed.*	car**ry** + **-es** = carr**ies** hur**ry** + **-ed** = hurr**ied**

Thinking It Through 1

Read the following sentences. Write them correctly on the lines provided. If the sentence is correct, write "correct as is."

1. The baseball team walked onto the feild.

_____

HINT   Think about which word does not look correct in the sentence. Then review the spelling rules.

2. The class decided to go swiming in the lake.

_____

HINT   Think about which word could be corrected by doubling the consonant before *-ing*.

3. Nelson was rakeing the leaves in our yard.

_____

4. Karen bought a turkey for our Thanksgiving dinner.

_____

5. Our dog always burys his bone in the garden.

_____

6. These boxes weigh a ton!

_____

A **singular noun** names one person, place, thing, or idea. A **plural noun** names more than one. Look at these spelling rules to see how to form plural nouns.

Rules	Singular	Plural
Add -*s* to most singular nouns.	one girl one kite	two girl**s** two kite**s**
Add -*es* to a singular noun that ends with *s, ss, ch, sh, zz,* or *x.*	one bus, a dress a bench one dish a whiz, a box	two bus**es**, two dress**es** some bench**es** many dish**es** two whizz**es**, two box**es**
If a noun ends with a vowel and *y*, add -*s*.	a monkey	three monkey**s**
If a noun ends with a consonant + *y*, change the *y* to *i* and add -*es*.	a family	four famil**ies**
If a noun ends with a vowel + *o*, add -*s*. If a noun ends with a consonant + *o*, add -*es*.	a rodeo one potato	some rodeo**s** two potato**es**
If a noun ends with *f* or *fe*, often change the *f* to *v* and add -*s* or -*es*.	one roof this scarf that leaf a knife	two roof**s** these scarf**s**/scar**ves** those lea**ves** some kni**ves**

You add -*s* or -*es* to form the plural of regular singular nouns. But **irregular plural nouns** do not form the plural by adding -*s* or -*es*. These words follow no spelling patterns. Here are some common irregular plural nouns.

man, woman	m**en**, wom**en**
child	child**ren**
foot, tooth	f**ee**t, t**ee**th

Some nouns have the same singular and plural forms. Look at this chart.

Singular	Plural
deer, sheep, series	deer, sheep, series

Thinking It Through 2

Read the following sentences. Write them correctly on the lines provided. If the sentence is correct, write "correct as is."

1. The foxs are hiding in the den.

   _____

   HINT Review the spelling rule for words that end in *x, s, ss, ch, sh,* and *zz.*

2. The toyes were left in the box.

   _____

   HINT Review the spelling rule for nouns that end in a vowel and *y.*

3. The sheep were in the meadow.

   _____

4. We decided to buy three tomatos.

   _____

5. I will talk to the childs in the class.

   _____

6. My grandparents took care of the babies.

   _____

Lesson Practice

This passage contains mistakes. Use the Reading Guide to help you find the mistakes.

Reading Guide

Which word in sentence 1 is not spelled correctly?

In sentence 4, is it correct to form the plural of *egg* by adding *-es*?

Are all of the words in sentence 7 spelled correctly? Is there one word that is misspelled?

After the Snow

(1) The snow started to fall on the rooves of the houses just as the sun was going down. (2) It continued all night long and did not stop until about noon the next day.

(3) Lori was so happy when school was closed for the day in her town and all the nearby citys. (4) She slept late that morning and had warm toast and fried <u>egges</u> for breakfast. (5) Then she set her sights on going out to play in the snow.

(6) She put on all the snow gear she could find. (7) She was hopeing that boots, gloves, a coat, a hat, snow pants, and two scarves would be enough. (8) As she <u>steped</u> outside, she saw that the branches were covered with snow. (9) The cold air touched her cheek.

(10) She stayed in the snow for more than an hour. (11) She shoveled the driveway for her parents and then built two <u>snowmans</u> for herself. (12) She loved the snow. (13) She wished it would snow every day!

(14) Lori knew that the next day would be a school day. (15) She <u>beleived</u> she was lucky to have a day off. (16) What a great day she was having playing in the snow!

Answer the following questions.

1. Which word is NOT spelled correctly in sentence 3 from paragraph 2?

   A. happy

   B. citys

   C. nearby

   D. closed

2. Read sentence 8 from paragraph 3.

   As she steped outside, she saw that the branches were covered with snow.

   What is the correct way to spell steped?

   A. stept

   B. stepd

   C. stepped

   D. steeped

3. Read sentence 11 from paragraph 4.

   She shoveled the driveway for her parents and then built two snowmans for herself.

   What is the correct way to spell snowmans?

   A. snowmans'

   B. snowmens

   C. snowmen's

   D. snowmen

4. Read sentence 15 from paragraph 5.

   She beleived she was lucky to have a day off.

   What is the correct way to spell beleived?

   A. belived

   B. believed

   C. believd

   D. beleivd

23 Articles and Abbreviations

3.10.g, 3.10.i

Getting the Idea

The words *a*, *an*, and *the* are special words called articles. An **article** is a word that introduces a noun. A **noun** is a word that names a person, place, thing, or idea. A noun can also name an animal.

A **definite article** is the word *the*. It refers to a specific noun. Read the following sentence.

The dog sat in the armchair.

In the sentence, the reader knows which dog and which chair. You use *the* to refer to a particular person, place, thing, idea, or animal.

An **indefinite article** can be the word *a* or *an*. These words refer to any one item in a group. They do not refer to a specific person, place, thing, idea, or animal. Use *a* if the next word begins with a consonant. Use *an* if the next word begins with a vowel. Read this example.

A dog sat in an armchair.

In this sentence, it does not matter which dog sat in which armchair.

Use *a* or *an* with singular nouns. Use *the* with singular and plural nouns. Look at the examples below.

Singular	Plural
a tree, an animal	
the tree, the animal	the trees, the animals

Thinking It Through 1

Read the following sentences. Write them correctly on the lines provided. If the sentence is correct, write "correct as is."

1. A teachers talked to Sara about her report.

_____

> HINT   Think about which article to use with plural nouns.

2. We saw a elephant at the zoo.

_____

> HINT   The word *elephant* begins with a vowel. Which article comes before a word that begins with a vowel?

3. I liked a sunset last night.

_____

4. She ate a pie at the bake sale.

_____

5. Josh hung the picture for me.

_____

6. Carmen ate a apple.

_____

An **abbreviation** is a shortened form of a word. Many abbreviations begin with a capital letter and end with a period. Use abbreviations only in special kinds of writing, such as memos or addresses. Look at the chart of common abbreviations.

	Abbreviations			
Titles	Doctor	**Dr.**		
	Senior	**Sr.**		
	Junior	**Jr.**		
	Mister	**Mr.**		
	Mrs.	(married woman)		
	Ms.	(married or single woman)		
Days	Monday	**Mon.**	Friday	**Fri.**
	Tuesday	**Tues.**	Saturday	**Sat.**
	Wednesday	**Wed.**	Sunday	**Sun.**
	Thursday	**Thurs.**		
Months	January	**Jan.**	September	**Sept.**
	February	**Feb.**	October	**Oct.**
	March	**Mar.**	November	**Nov.**
	April	**Apr.**	December	**Dec.**
	August	**Aug.**		
Addresses	Avenue	**Ave.**	Street	**St.**
	Road	**Rd.**	Drive	**Dr.**
Some state names used with Zip codes	California	**CA**	Texas	**TX**
	New York	**NY**	Virginia	**VA**
Other abbreviations	Post Office	**P.O.**	United Nations	**UN**
	Company	**Co.**	United States	**U.S.**
	inch, inches	**in.**	foot, feet	**ft.**

Some abbreviations, such as UN, use all capital letters and no periods. Others, such as A.M and P.M., are shortened forms of the Latin words they came from. Use abbreviations correctly. This will make it easier for your readers to understand your writing.

Thinking It Through 2

Read the following sentences. Write them correctly on the lines provided. Use the correct abbreviation for the underlined word. If the sentence is correct, write "correct as is."

1. Ask <u>Mister</u> Rosen about the homework.

_____

HINT The abbreviation for *Mister* is the one we use before a man's last name.

2. Meet me at noon on Center <u>Road</u>.

_____

HINT What is the correct abbreviation for this street name?

3. <u>Doctor</u> Peggy Chang will answer your questions.

_____

4. The <u>United States</u> government collects taxes.

_____

5. The test will be on <u>Thursday</u> next week.

_____

6. School begins on <u>Sept.</u> 6.

_____

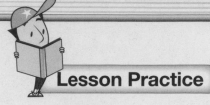

Lesson Practice

This passage contains mistakes. Use the Reading Guide to help you find the mistakes.

Reading Guide

Does it make sense to say *a school shows* or *the school shows* in sentence 2? Why?

What month is *Feb.* an abbreviation for in sentence 4?

In the last sentence, how do you write the two-letter abbreviation for *New York* correctly?

The Dance Lesson

(1) Tasha had always wanted to learn to dance. (2) She would watch her older sister dance at <u>a school shows</u>. (3) She would sit in a audience and say to herself, "That's what I want to do."

(4) On <u>Feb.</u> 15, her mom brought her to her first dance class. (5) It started at 9:00 A.M. on Saturday.

(6) The dance class was held at a small studio on Grayson Av. and Fifth St. (7) The studio was above a pizza shop. (8) Tasha brought an umbrella the first day because it was raining. (9) She met her teacher, Ms. Long, at the door. (10) The teacher took Tasha's coat and umbrella, and they talked.

(11) Then it was time to dance! (12) Tasha and Ms. Long each put on the pair of ballet slippers and got to work. (13) Tasha watched her teacher carefully. (14) She did everything Ms. Long did. (15) Tasha knew she could be a great dancer if she tried very hard. (16) She would practice every day. (17) She might even become the best dancer in the <u>Ny</u> Ballet.

Answer the following questions.

1. What is the correct way to write sentence 3 from paragraph 1?

   A. She would sit in an audience's and say to herself, "That's what I want to do."

   B. She would sit in a audiences and say to herself, "That's what I want to do."

   C. She would sit in the audience and say to herself, "That's what I want to do."

   D. correct as is

2. What is the correct way to write sentence 5 from paragraph 2?

   A. It started at 9:00 A.m. on Saturday.

   B. It started at 9:00 A.M. on Saturday.

   C. It started at 9:00 am on Saturday.

   D. It started at 9:00 aM on Saturday.

3. What is the correct way to write sentence 6 from paragraph 3?

   A. The dance class was held at a small studio on Grayson Ave. and Fifth St.

   B. The dance class was held at a small studio on Grayson Av. and Fifth Sts.

   C. The dance class was held at a small studio on Grayson Aven. and Fifth Str.

   D. The dance class was held at a small studio on Grayson AVE and Fifth ST.

4. What is the correct way to write sentence 12 from the last paragraph?

   A. Tasha and Ms. Long each put on an pair of ballet slippers and got to work.

   B. Tasha and Ms. Long each put on a pair of ballet slippers and got to work.

   C. Tasha and Ms. Long each put on the pair of ballet slipper and got to work.

   D. correct as is

24 Possessives and Contractions

3.10.e, 3.10.h

Getting the Idea

A **pronoun** is a word that takes the place of a **noun**. Many pronouns take the place of a noun that is the subject of the sentence. The **subject** tells *who* or *what* the sentence is about. Read the sentences below.

Dan eats grapes.   **He** eats grapes.
Holly runs races.   **She** runs races.
A **hammer** is useful.   **It** is useful.

A pronoun can also come after a **verb** that shows action. An **action verb** tells what the subject of a sentence does. A pronoun can also come after words such as *with*, *for*, *at*, and *to*. Look at how the nouns in these sentences are replaced by pronouns.

Carl watches **Bob**.   Carl watches **him**.
Mom helps **Dora**.   Mom helps **her**.
Dad gives the book to **Pedro**.   Dad gives the book to **him**.

Read this chart of singular pronouns. Look at the two kinds of pronouns.

Pronouns that take the place of the subject	Pronouns that come after action verbs
I	me
you	you
he, she, it	him, her, it

Another kind of pronoun is a possessive pronoun. A **possessive pronoun** shows *who* or *what* has or owns something. It shows ownership. There are two kinds of possessive pronouns. You use one kind before nouns. The other kind stands alone.

Read this chart of singular possessive pronouns. See how two kinds of possessive pronouns are used.

Pronouns used before nouns	Pronouns used alone
My pen is on the desk.	**Mine** is on the desk.
Your pencil is on the floor.	**Yours** is on the floor.
His coat is in the closet.	**His** is in the closet.
Her computer is at home.	**Hers** is at home.
Its fur is brown.	**Its** is brown.

Sometimes, you can use a **singular possessive noun** to show ownership. You add an **apostrophe** and s ('s) to a singular noun to make it possessive.

Singular Nouns	Singular Possessive Nouns
The pen belongs to Roy.	**Roy's** pen
the computer Dad owns	**Dad's** computer
the leash of the dog	the **dog's** leash

An apostrophe can also take the place of the missing letter or letters in a contraction. A **contraction** is the short word you make when you combine two words. A contraction can join a pronoun and a verb.

I am	I'm
you are	you're
it is	it's
I will, you will	I'll, you'll
he will, she will, it will	he'll, she'll, it'll
you have	you've
you would	you'd

A contraction can also join a verb with the word *not*.

is not, are not	isn't, aren't
was not, were not	wasn't, weren't
does not, do not, did not	doesn't, don't, didn't
cannot, could not	can't, couldn't
would not, should not, will not	wouldn't, shouldn't, won't

Thinking It Through

Read the following paragraph, and then answer the question that follows.

My father's friend is very funny. He tells jokes and plays tricks on me. I like the way he makes people laugh. My dad says he'll always be friends with him. I wonder if that means he will be making me laugh for many years to come.

Which word from the paragraph is an example of a singular possessive noun? Tell how you know.

_____

_____

_____

_____

_____

HINT You add an apostrophe and *s* ('s) to a singular noun to make it possessive.

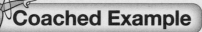

Coached Example

Read the passage and answer the questions.

I left my homework at school today. I should have checked my notebook to make sure I had everything I needed. My science project was due today and that made me forget my usual routine.

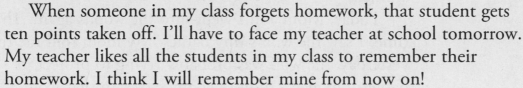

I was nervous about the project, so I could not stop thinking about it. My teacher thought I'd done a great job, so I'm proud about that. I just couldn't remember to bring my homework home!

When someone in my class forgets homework, that student gets ten points taken off. I'll have to face my teacher at school tomorrow. My teacher likes all the students in my class to remember their homework. I think I will remember mine from now on!

---

1. Which word in sentence 1 is a possessive pronoun?

   A. I

   B. my

   C. at

   D. today

   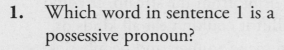 A possessive pronoun shows that someone has or owns something.

2. Which of the following is NOT a contraction with a pronoun?

   A. I'm

   B. I'll

   C. couldn't

   D. I'd

   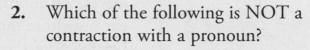 Think about which contraction joins a verb with the word *not*.

Lesson Practice

Use the Reading Guide to help you understand the passage.

Reading Guide

Are there any pronouns in paragraph 1?

In paragraph 3, what two words does the contraction *I'll* take the place of?

What pronouns can you find in the last sentence?

The Life of a Wolf

A wolf is a beautiful animal. It is a member of the dog family. People like wolves, but a wolf can be dangerous to people.

Yesterday, I saw a wolf in the woods near my house. It had dark, beautiful eyes. Mom told me not to go near it. She said that wolves can attack people.

I know <u>I'll</u> always remember seeing that wolf. I don't think you'd ever forget seeing such a strong, beautiful animal.

Today, Mom and I went into the woods again. This time, I saw the wolf's tiny babies. My mom told me that yesterday, the wolf was probably trying to protect its babies. <u>I'm</u> glad I <u>didn't</u> get any closer to that wolf!

I think the woods near my house would make a great home for animals. Animals could hide under fallen leaves. An animal could drink from the stream. It could eat nuts from the trees. But it couldn't eat all kinds of berries. Some berries can make animals and people sick. I think if I were a wolf, <u>I'd</u> like living in the woods near my home.

Answer the following questions.

1. Which pronoun in paragraph 2 shows who or what has or owns something?

    A. my

    B. it

    C. me

    D. I

2. Read this sentence from paragraph 3.

    I don't think you'd ever forget seeing such a strong, beautiful animal.

    Which word in the sentence is a contraction with a pronoun?

    A. I

    B. you'd

    C. ever

    D. don't

3. Read this sentence from paragraph 4.

    I'm glad I <u>didn't</u> get any closer to that wolf!

    Which words do the two contractions take the place of?

    A. I am, does not

    B. I will, did not

    C. I am, did not

    D. I am, do not

4. Read the last sentence from the passage.

    I think if I were a wolf, I'd like living in the woods near my home.

    Which two words does the contraction take the place of in the sentence?

    A. I did

    B. I would

    C. I had

    D. I do

5. Read this sentence from paragraph 4.

    My mom told me that yesterday, the wolf was probably trying to protect its babies.

    Which words in the sentence are possessive pronouns?

25 Verb Tenses

3.10.d

Getting the Idea

A **verb** is a word that shows action or a state of being. Verbs form the main part of a sentence. An **action verb** tells what someone or something does. For example, the word *run* is a verb. It tells the action in the sentence. Read the sentences below.

> I **run** every day.

> Eileen **drinks** orange juice.

> Jamie and Rebecca **ride** their bikes to school.

The words in bold (or dark) print are all action verbs. They show the action in each sentence. Verbs usually come *after* the subject of a sentence. The subject shows *who* or *what* is doing the action.

Not all verbs show action. The verb *be* does not show action. It tells what someone or something is or is like. The verbs *am*, *is*, *are*, *was*, and *were* are all forms of the verb *be*. Read the sentences below.

> I **am** sleepy.

> Eileen **is** happy.

> Jamie and Rebecca **are** tired.

The words in bold (or dark) print are all forms of the verb *be*. They do not show action. They tell what the subject is or is like.

Thinking It Through 1

Read the following sentences. Write them correctly on the lines provided. If the sentence is correct, write "correct as is."

1. Dale a letter wrote.

_____

> **HINT** Verbs are usually action words. In general, verbs come after the subject of a sentence.

2. My sister tall is.

_____

> **HINT** Verbs can also tell what someone or something is or is like. What is the subject? How is it being described?

3. My mother questioned me.

_____

4. The cat happy was.

_____

5. My teeth I brush every day.

_____

6. I am the tallest boy in the class.

_____

Verb tense shows when an action happens. An action can happen in the past, the present, or the future. **Past tense** verbs show an action that has already happened. **Present tense** verbs show an action that happens now. **Future tense** verbs show an action that will happen in the future. The chart below shows some examples.

Verb Tenses

Past Tense	Present Tense	Future Tense
I **walked** to the store.	I **walk** to the store.	I **will walk** to the store.
Amy **baked** cookies.	Amy **bakes** cookies.	Amy **will bake** cookies.
Dad and Mom **cooked** eggs and bacon.	Dad and Mom **cook** eggs and bacon.	Dad and Mom **will cook** eggs and bacon.
You **touched** the statue.	You **touch** the statue.	You **will touch** the statue.

Writers must use the same verb tense throughout their writing. If a writer shifts tense for no reason, it can confuse the reader. The one time a writer can change tense is when writing dialogue.

Most verbs are **regular verbs**. In the past tense, they end in *-d* or *-ed*. However, some verbs are irregular. They do not follow the rules in the chart above. An **irregular verb** does not form the past tense by adding *-d* or *-ed*. The verbs *to be*, *to run*, and *to drink* are irregular verbs. In the past tense, the verb *to be* becomes *was* or *were*. The verb *run* becomes *ran*. The verb *drink* becomes *drank*. There are many irregular verbs in English. By using them in your writing, you will get to know their different verb forms.

Thinking It Through 2

Read the following sentences. Write them correctly on the lines provided. If the sentence is correct, write "correct as is."

1. Tomorrow I finished my homework.

_____

> **HINT** Verbs can be in the present, the past, or the future tense. Tense tells when an action happens. Decide which tense this sentence should be, and then fix the verb.

2. Dad will order Chinese food last night.

_____

> **HINT** Look for clue words that tell you when the action happens. Does the verb tense match the time of the action?

3. Yesterday they run a race.

_____

4. She placed second in last week's race.

_____

5. I drinked a bottle of water after soccer practice.

_____

6. I will be on time tomorrow morning.

_____

Lesson Practice

This passage contains mistakes. Use the Reading Guide to help you find the mistakes.

Reading Guide

What is the present tense of *dropped* in sentence 5?

Look at the irregular verbs *went*, *was*, *had*, *bought*, and *let* in paragraph 1. Do you see more irregular verbs in paragraph 3?

In which tense is the verb *showed* in sentence 8?

How do regular verbs form the past tense?

My First Subway Ride

(1) Years ago, I <u>went</u> on a subway in Boston. (2) It <u>was</u> called the "T." (3) You <u>had</u> to pay to ride. (4) My parents <u>bought</u> tokens for all of us. (5) I <u>dropped</u> mine into the slot of a machine. (6) That <u>let</u> me through the turnstile and onto the platform.

(7) While we waited for our train to arrive, I looked at a map on the wall. (8) It <u>showed</u> all the subway lines of the "T." (9) The train at the station finally arrived.

(10) We got on the train. (11) The train will tremble as it moved. (12) It made a lot of creaking noises.

(13) We rode for about ten minutes when all of a sudden, the train stopped. (14) What was happening? (15) The lights went out. (16) Would we be stuck on this train forever? (17) We waited for what seemed like a long time. (18) But it was probably less than a minute.

Answer the following questions.

1. Read sentence 1 from paragraph 1.

   Years ago, I <u>went</u> on a subway in Boston.

   Which is the verb in the sentence?

   A. I

   B. on

   C. went

   D. subway

2. Read sentence 9 from paragraph 2.

   The train at the station finally arrived.

   What is the correct way to write this sentence?

   A. The train finally at the station arrived.

   B. The train at the station arrived finally.

   C. The train finally arrived at the station.

   D. Finally, the train at the station arrived.

3. Read sentence 11 from paragraph 3.

   The train will tremble as it moved.

   What is the correct way to write this sentence?

   A. The train trembles as it moved.

   B. The train trembled as it moved.

   C. The train will trembled as it moves.

   D. The train trembles as it will move.

4. Read sentence 18 from the last paragraph.

   But it was probably less than a minute.

   Which is the verb in the sentence?

   A. it

   B. was

   C. less

   D. minute

26 Sentence Structure

3.10.a–c, 3.10.f

Getting the Idea

A **complete sentence** is a group of words that tells a complete idea. It has a subject and a verb. The **subject** tells *who* or *what* the sentence is about. It is usually a noun or a pronoun. The **verb** usually tells what action the subject does.

> The cat plays.

Cat is the subject of the sentence. It is what the sentence is about. *Plays* is the verb. It tells the action that the subject (cat) does.

A complete sentence starts with a capital letter and has an end mark. An **end mark** is a **punctuation mark** at the end of a sentence. Look at these different kinds of sentences and end marks.

One kind of sentence makes a statement. It ends with a **period (.)**.

> My dad likes sports.

One kind of sentence asks a question. It ends with a **question mark (?)**.

> When does the game start?

One kind of sentence shows surprise or strong feeling. It ends with an **exclamation point (!)**.

> What a great game this is!

A **compound subject** has two or more simple subjects joined by the word *and*. Sometimes the word *I* is part of a compound subject.

> Wanda and I are friends.

Wanda and I is the compound subject. *Are* is the verb. Now read this.

> Dogs, cats, and fish make good pets.

Use a comma to separate three or more items in a series.

Thinking It Through 1

Read the following sentences. Write them correctly on the lines provided. If the sentence is correct, write "correct as is."

1. Where is the cat.

_____

HINT Think about the different kinds of end marks and what they mean.

2. My book coat and boots.

_____

HINT Remember that a complete sentence must have a subject and a verb.

3. Iris sings in the concert.

_____

4. go to the store.

_____

5. Do you want to sing?

_____

6. The paper and pencil in the drawer.

_____

It is important to make your writing interesting for your readers. Your writing will be more interesting if you vary sentence structure. **Varying sentence structure** means

- using different kinds of sentences.
- using some simple subjects and some compound subjects.
- using sentences that are long and short.
- combining short, choppy sentences.
- using transition words, such as *now*, *then*, or *however*, to connect ideas.

Read the example below.

> Mom bought eggs. I bought bread. Mom bought milk.
> I bought butter. We bought fruit and jam. It's going to
> be a good breakfast.

The paragraph can be made better by making the sentences less choppy. You can combine short, choppy sentences by using a compound subject. Remember to use a comma to separate three or more items in a series. Also use different kinds of sentences. Read the paragraph below.

> Mom and I bought eggs, bread, milk, and butter. Then we
> bought fruit and jam. What a great breakfast it's going to be!

Now the sentences about what Mom and I bought do not repeat the subject and verb. The third sentence now has a transition word (*then*) to connect ideas. The last sentence is not another statement. It's an exclamation.

Thinking It Through 2

Read the following sentences. Write them correctly on the lines provided. If the sentence is correct, write "correct as is."

1. We will read. We will write. We will sing songs.

    _____

    HINT   The sentences are too choppy. Rewrite them so that you do not have to repeat the subject and verb.

2. Tanya milked the cows. I milked the cows.

    _____

    HINT   How can you combine the two sentences into one sentence?

3. Mr. Garcia and his daughter painted the house.

    _____

4. Mike will be there. Danny will be there. Max will be there.

    _____

5. Will you pass the salt? Will you pass the pepper?

    _____

6. Awilda loves animals and has two dogs.

    _____

Lesson Practice

This passage contains mistakes. Use the Reading Guide to help you find the mistakes.

Reading Guide

Does paragraph 1 use different kinds of sentences?

Which sentences sound choppy in paragraph 3?

Which choppy sentences can you combine in paragraph 4?

What is the best way to combine sentences 18, 19, and 20 in paragraph 5?

Our Bake Sale

(1) Do you like sweet treats? (2) Join us for a bake sale at our school. (3) There will be plenty of sweet treats for you to enjoy.

(4) The money from the bake sale will go toward buying new books for the school. (5) As you know, we really need new books.

(6) Ms. Weston will bring brownies. (7) She will bring cookies. (8) She will bring granola bars. (9) Mr. Sato will bring cupcakes. (10) Mrs. Ng will bring cupcakes.

(11) If you would like to bake, please call Mrs. Park. (12) If you would like to sell food, please call Mrs. Park. (13) If you would like to collect money, please call Mrs. Park. (14) For anything else, please call Ms. Canton. (15) Mrs. Park and Ms. Canton are in charge of the bake sale.

(16) Our third-grade class hopes to earn a lot of money from the bake sale. (17) We can use a lot of new books and supplies in the classroom. (18) We will buy fiction books. (19) We will buy nonfiction books. (20) We will start a classroom library.

(21) Can you come to our bake sale? (22) It will start this Thursday at 9:00 A.M. (23) It will end this Thursday at 4:00 P.M. (24) Please join us. (25) What a great bake sale it's going to be!

Answer the following questions.

1. What is the BEST way to write sentences 6, 7, and 8 from paragraph 3?

   A. Ms. Weston will bring brownies. Ms. Weston will bring cookies. Ms. Weston will bring granola bars.

   B. Ms. Weston will bring brownies. She will bring cookies, and she will bring granola bars.

   C. Ms. Weston will bring brownies, cookies, and granola bars.

   D. Ms. Weston will bring brownies and cookies, and she will bring granola bars.

2. How would you combine sentences 9 and 10 from paragraph 3 into one sentence?

   A. Mr. Sato will bring cupcakes, and Mrs. Ng will bring cupcakes.

   B. Mr. Sato and Mrs. Ng will bring cupcakes.

   C. Mr. Sato will bring cupcakes, and she will bring cupcakes.

   D. He will bring cupcakes, and she will bring cupcakes.

3. Which sentence from the passage asks a question?

   A. Please join us.

   B. Do you like sweet treats?

   C. We will start a classroom library.

   D. What a great bake sale it's going to be!

4. Which sentence from the passage has a compound subject?

   A. Can you come to our bake sale?

   B. Ms. Weston will bring brownies.

   C. Mrs. Park and Ms. Canton are in charge of the bake sale.

   D. We can use a lot of new books and supplies in the classroom.

4 Review

This passage contains mistakes. Read the passage and answer the questions that follow.

Giraffes

(1) Giraffes live in Africa. (2) They are a tallest land animal. (3) A full-grown male giraffe can be up to eighteen <u>feet</u> tall. (4) A giraffe's neck. (5) Giraffes have seven neck bones just like humans. (6) But for the giraffe, each one can be more than ten inches long. (7) Its legs are about six feet long, too. (8) What holds up those long legs? (9) A giraffe has really big feet. (10) Each one is about twelve inches across. (11) A large giraffe weighs a lot, too. (12) A male giraffe can be about 3,000 pounds. (13) A female weighs about half that. (14) Giraffes have small horns on top of their head. (15) Scientists believe the horns are used to protect the giraffes' head in fights.

(16) It takes a lot of food to feed a large animal. (17) Giraffes can eat up to seventy-five pounds of food every day. (18) Their favorite leafs are from thorny acacia trees. (19) The thorns don't bother the giraffes as they eat. (20) They use their long tongues to reach around most of the thorns. (21) A giraffes tongue is about eighteen inches long.

(22) Giraffes are social animals. (23) They travel in herds. (24) Giraffe herds are not very organized. (25) A herd can be made up of all males, all females, or a mix. (26) The herds do not have one special leader.

(27) Because giraffes are so big, they do not hide from their enemies. (28) Lions leopards and crocodiles hunt them. (29) But a giraffe can defend itself with its powerful kick. (30) Giraffes can also run quickly to escape. (31) They can run up to thirty-five miles an hour!

(32) A giraffe's coat has a spotted pattern. (33) It looks like the pattern of leopards. (34) In ancient times, Romans called giraffes "camelopards." (35) They described giraffes as having a camel's body and a leopard's spots. (36) Giraffes and leopards do not have much in common. (37) They are both mammals, but the two animals are natural enemies. (38) Even though the leopard is much smaller than the giraffe, it's the leopard that hunts its taller neighbor.

1. What is the correct abbreviation for <u>feet</u> in sentence 3 from paragraph 1?

   A. fe.

   B. ft.

   C. foot

   D. ft

2. What is the correct way to write sentence 2 from paragraph 1?

   A. They are an tallest land animal.

   B. They are the tallest land animal.

   C. They are a tallest land animals.

   D. They are that tallest land animals.

3. Read sentence 18 from paragraph 2.

   Their favorite leafs are from thorny acacia trees.

   Which word from this sentence is NOT spelled correctly?

   A. leafs

   B. Their

   C. thorny

   D. trees

4. What is the correct way to write sentence 21 from paragraph 2?

   A. A giraffe's tongue is about 18 inches long.

   B. A giraffes' tongue is about 18 inches long.

   C. A giraffe tong is about 18 ins. long.

   D. A giraffe tung is about 18 in long.

5. Which word from the last paragraph is a possessive pronoun?

   A. giraffe's

   B. it's

   C. It

   D. its

6. Read sentence 24 from paragraph 3.

   Giraffe herds are not very organized.

   Which transition word could you add to the beginning of the sentence?

   A. However

   B. Later

   C. Soon

   D. Before

7. Read these words from sentence 4 of paragraph 1.

   A giraffe's neck.

   How could you make these words into a complete sentence?

   A. A giraffe's neck is very.

   B. A giraffe's neck long.

   C. A giraffe's neck very long is.

   D. A giraffe's neck is very long.

8. What is the correct way to write sentence 28 from paragraph 4?

   A. Lions, leopards and crocodiles, hunt them.

   B. Lions leopards, and crocodiles hunt them.

   C. Lions, leopards, and crocodiles hunt them.

   D. Lion's, leopard's, and crocodile's hunt them.

This passage contains mistakes. Read the passage and answer the questions that follow.

Skyline Caverns

(1) Emma was excited because her class was taking a trip to Skyline Caverns. (2) The class was studying rocks in earth science. (3) Emma loved rocks. (4) She wanted to be a geologist when she grew up. (5) She had rocks from the beach that were worn smooth by the water. (6) She had once believed that mermaids carried the smooth rocks to shore for her to find. (7) Emma also had rocks with sharp edges that she <u>recieved</u> from a catalog.

(8) Once, Emma's uncle Raymond had brought her a orange rock from Utah. (9) He said there were lots of colorful rocks there. (10) Emma wanted to see Utah someday, but that day she was thinking about Skyline Caverns.

(11) Emma had read all about Skyline Caverns. (12) She couldn't wait to see the stalactites and stalagmites. (13) She wanted to see the icy, hanging rocks. (14) Her friend Jerry was nervous. (15) He didn't like dark places. (16) Jerry had a vivid imagination.

(17) "What if there are millions of vampire bats in there?" Jerry exclaimed.

(18) "Don't worry, Jerry," said Emma. (19) "Bats are in the caves, but they were not vampire bats."

(20) Jerry still looked nervous. (21) "It might be really dark in there. (22) Shouldn't we have brought flashlights?"

(23) "The main part of the tour has lights. (24) Uncle Raymond and I read it in the brochure. (25) It's going to be fun, Jerry." (26) Emma smiled, and Jerry smiled back. (27) Emma was excited about the things she would see. (28) She would see minerals hanging rocks and wonderful colors.

(29) The school bus was on Rivermont <u>Drive</u> now. (30) Soon, it would stop at Skyline Caverns. (31) When the bus stopped, the tour guide began directing the students to the cave entrance. (32) Emma moved to the front of the line, pulling Jerry with her. (33) Emmas excitement was rising. (34) She could also see a tiny smile in the corner of Jerry's mouth. (35) It was going to be a great day!

9. Read sentence 1 from paragraph 1.

Emma was excited because her class was taking a trip to Skyline Caverns.

Which word from the sentence is a possessive pronoun?

A. Emma

B. her

C. class

D. taking

10. What is the correct way to spell <u>recieved</u> in sentence 7 from paragraph 1?

A. receivd

B. received

C. resieved

D. ricieved

11. Read sentence 8 from paragraph 2.

Once, Emma's uncle Raymond had brought her a orange rock from Utah.

Which part of the sentence contains an error?

A. Once, Emma's uncle Raymond

B. had brought her

C. a orange rock

D. from Utah

12. Read sentence 33 from the last paragraph.

Emmas excitement was rising.

What is the correct way to write this sentence?

A. Emma excitement was rising.

B. Emmas excitement is rising.

C. Emmas' excitement was rising.

D. Emma's excitement was rising.

13. Read sentence 19 from paragraph 5.

    "Bats are in the caves, but they were not vampire bats."

    What is the correct way to write this sentence?

    A. "Bats aren't in the caves, but they weren't vampire bats."

    B. "Bats were in the caves, but they was not vampire bats."

    C. "Bats were in the caves, but they are not vampire bats."

    D. "Bats are in the caves, but they are not vampire bats."

14. Which sentence in the passage has a compound subject?

    A. sentence 12

    B. sentence 24

    C. sentence 25

    D. sentence 34

15. What is the correct way to write sentence 28?

    A. She would see minerals, hanging rocks, and wonderful colors.

    B. She would see minerals, hanging rocks and wonderful, colors.

    C. She would see minerals hanging rocks, and wonderful colors.

    D. She would see minerals, hanging, rocks, and wonderful colors.

16. Read sentence 29 from the last paragraph.

    The school bus was on Rivermont <u>Drive</u> now.

    What is the correct abbreviation for <u>Drive</u>?

    A. Dri.

    B. Dve.

    C. Dr.

    D. DRV.

Glossary

abbreviation a shortened form of a word (Lesson 23)

action verb a verb that shows action and tells what the subject of a sentence does (Lessons 24–26)

affix a group of letters (or word part) that is added to the beginning or end of a root or root word (Lesson 3)

antonyms words that have opposite or almost opposite meanings (Lessons 4, 6)

apostrophe (') a punctuation mark that is used to show possession or a missing letter (or letters) in a contraction (Lesson 24)

article the words *a*, *an*, and *the,* which introduce a noun (Lesson 23)

audience the readers of an author's work (Lessons 9, 17)

author's purpose the reason an author writes something (Lessons 9, 17)

autobiography a true story about a person's life, written by that person (Lessons 9, 12)

bibliography a list of the resources used for a research report (Lesson 21)

biography a true story about a person's life, written by someone else (Lessons 9, 12)

bold print type that is darker than the rest of the words (Lesson 16)

caption a short title or description that usually comes below a picture and tells what the picture is about (Lesson 16)

cause the reason something happens (Lesson 6)

cause and effect a pattern that shows how one event causes another event to happen (Lesson 6)

character a made-up person or animal in a story or play (Lessons 12, 13, 18)

chart a graphic feature, usually of columns and rows, that gives information quickly, clearly, and easily (Lesson 16)

compare to show how two or more people or things are alike (Lessons 6, 12, 18)

compare and contrast to show how two or more people or things are alike and how they are different (Lessons 6, 12, 18)

complete sentence a group of words that tells a complete idea and has a subject and a verb (Lesson 26)

compound subject a subject that has two or more simple subjects, joined by the word *and*; sometimes, the word *I* is part of a compound subject (Lesson 26)

conclusion a decision you make about what you have read based on the inferences you made during reading; often the last sentence in a piece of writing that restates or sums up the main idea (Lessons 15, 19)

confirm to check if your prediction about a story is correct (Lesson 14)

conflict another word for a problem in a story that usually a character must solve (Lesson 13)

content area a subject of study, such as science, math, or social studies (Lesson 7)

context clues surrounding words in a sentence or in nearby sentences that can help you figure out the meaning of an unfamiliar word (Lesson 6)

contraction the short word that is made when two words are combined (Lesson 24)

contrast to show how two or more people or things are different (Lessons 6, 12, 18)

definite article the word *the* before a specific singular or plural noun (Lesson 23)

definition the exact meaning of a word (Lessons 6, 8)

dialogue the words that the characters say to each other in a story or play (Lessons 9, 18)

dictionary a book or an online source that gives the definition (or meaning) of a word (Lesson 8)

draft one of the first versions of a writer's work (Lesson 20)

edit to fix a draft by correcting mistakes in grammar, spelling, capitalization, and punctuation (Lesson 20)

effect the result of a cause (Lesson 6)

end mark a punctuation mark, such as a period, a question mark, or an exclamation point, at the end of a sentence (Lesson 26)

entertain the author's purpose for writing a story, a play, a poem, or another work of fiction that will amuse readers (Lessons 9, 17)

example a specific type of something (Lesson 6)

exclamation point (!) an end mark that shows surprise or strong feeling; also known as *exclamation mark* (Lesson 26)

expository writing nonfiction writing that gives facts and information about a topic, and explains ideas; also known as *informational writing* (Lesson 18)

fable a story that has animal characters and teaches a moral, or lesson (Lesson 9)

fact information that can be proved to be true (Lesson 9)

fairy tale a story about magic deeds that begins "Once upon a time" and may have a king, queen, prince, or princess as characters (Lesson 9)

fiction writing that describes imaginary people, places, and events (Lessons 9, 10, 12)

first-person point of view the viewpoint of a narrator who uses the pronoun *I* to tell a story (Lesson 12)

folktale a story handed down by word of mouth from one generation to another that often explains how or why something came into being (Lesson 9)

future tense a verb form that shows an action that will happen in the future (Lesson 25)

glossary a list of words and their meanings, usually at the back of a nonfiction book (Lessons 7, 8)

graphic features elements, such as pictures, maps, diagrams, or charts, that organize and explain information in a visual way (Lesson 16)

graphic organizer a visual aid, such as a sequence chart, a Venn diagram, or a web, that helps writers plan and organize their ideas for writing (Lessons 18, 19)

headings words that name what a section of a passage is about (Lesson 16)

homophones words that are pronounced the same but have different meanings and often different spellings (Lesson 4)

indefinite article the word *a* or *an* that introduces a singular noun (Lesson 23)

index a list in alphabetical (ABC) order of topics in a nonfiction book and the page on which each topic can be found (Lesson 16)

inference a guess that you make while you read, based on what the author tells you and on your own knowledge and experiences (Lesson 15)

inform the author's purpose for writing some kinds of nonfiction that gives facts and information, and explains ideas (Lessons 9, 17, 18)

informational writing nonfiction writing that gives facts and information about a topic, and explains ideas; also known as *expository writing* (Lesson 18)

irregular plural noun a noun that does not form the plural by adding *-s* or *-es* (Lesson 22)

irregular verb a verb that does not form the past tense by adding -d or -ed (Lesson 25)

main idea what the passage is mostly about (Lessons 11, 19)

meaning clues words that help you understand the meaning of another word (Lesson 5)

multisyllabic words words with more than one syllable (Lesson 2)

narrative writing writing that tells a story (Lesson 18)

narrator the person who tells the story (Lesson 18)

nonfiction writing that gives you facts and information, and explains ideas (Lessons 9, 12)

noun a word that names a person, place, thing, animal, or idea (Lessons 23, 24)

opinion a statement that is usually based on the author's feelings or beliefs (Lessons 9, 17)

organization the order in which sentences are arranged in a paragraph or passage (Lesson 20)

outline a list of ideas in the order that you plan to write about them (Lesson 21)

past tense a verb form that shows that an action has already happened (Lesson 25)

period (.) an end mark that comes at the end of a sentence that makes a statement (Lesson 26)

persuade the author's purpose for writing that tries to get an audience to agree with his or her opinion, or to think or act in a certain way (Lessons 9, 17)

phonetics the way a word (or word part) sounds (Lesson 5)

plot the sequence of events in the beginning, middle, and end of a story (Lessons 12, 13, 18)

plural noun a noun that names more than one person, place, thing, animal, or idea (Lesson 22)

poetry fiction written in lines that uses rhythm, stress, creative language, and often rhyme (Lesson 9)

point of view the viewpoint from which the narrator tells a story (Lesson 18)

possessive pronoun a pronoun that shows *who* or *what* has or owns something (Lesson 24)

prediction a guess about what might happen in a story (Lesson 14)

prefix a group of letters (or word part) that is added to the beginning of a root or root word (Lesson 3)

present tense a verb form that shows an action that happens now (Lesson 25)

prewriting the activities done before writing, such as making a list of topics or a chart of ideas (Lesson 18)

problem the conflict in the plot of a story that usually a character must solve (Lessons 13, 18)

problem and solution a pattern that presents a problem, or conflict, and shows how it is solved (Lessons 13, 18)

pronoun a word that takes the place of a noun (Lesson 24)

publish to let others read the final draft of your writing (Lesson 20)

punctuation mark any of the marks used in writing to separate sentences or sentence parts, such as a period or comma (Lesson 26)

question mark (?) an end mark that comes at the end of a question (Lesson 26)

regular verb a verb that forms the past tense by adding -*d* or -*ed*. (Lesson 25)

research to get facts and information from resources such as books, encyclopedias, newspapers, and Web sites (Lesson 21)

research report writing that is based on information from trustworthy print or online resources (Lesson 21)

resolution the end of a story when the problem is solved (Lesson 13)

resource any material, such as an encyclopedia, that helps a writer find information (Lesson 21)

restatement another way to say the same thing (Lesson 6)

revise to change a prediction you made while reading or a draft after writing (Lessons 14, 20)

root the main part of a word (Lesson 3)

root word a complete word that is formed from a root (Lesson 3)

scan to read a passage quickly to look for key words or terms to find specific information; the words *skim* and *scan* are often used together (Lesson 11)

sequence chart a graphic organizer that shows the order in which events happen in a story (Lesson 18)

setting where and when a story takes place (Lessons 12, 13, 18)

setting a purpose the reason someone reads something (Lesson 9)

singular noun a noun that names one person, place, thing, animal, or idea (Lesson 22)

singular possessive noun a noun showing that something belongs to a person or thing (Lesson 24)

skim to read a passage quickly to get the general idea; the words *skim* and *scan* are often used together (Lesson 11)

solution the way a problem is solved in a story (Lessons 13, 18)

spelling the correct way of ordering letters in words (Lesson 22)

structure clues punctuation marks or word arrangements that give hints about the meaning of a word or an idea (Lesson 5)

subject the part of a sentence that tells *who* or *what* the sentence is about (Lessons 24, 26)

suffix a group of letters (or word part) that is added to the end of a root or root word (Lesson 3)

summarize to state the main idea of a text and tell only the most important information (Lesson 11)

supporting details facts, examples, or descriptions that give information about the main idea (Lessons 11, 20)

syllable a small unit of sound (Lesson 2)

synonyms words that have the same or almost the same meanings (Lessons 4, 6)

table of contents pages in the front of a book that show the name of each chapter and the page on which each chapter begins (Lesson 16)

text features elements, including the title, headings, captions, table of contents, and index, that explain, add to, or organize the text to help you find or understand information (Lesson 16)

thesaurus a book or an online source that gives synonyms and antonyms for words (Lesson 8)

third-person point of view the viewpoint of a narrator who uses *he* or *she* to tell a story (Lesson 12)

title the name of a book, story, or another type of writing that tells what it is about (Lesson 16)

topic sentence a sentence that tells the main idea of a paragraph or a passage and is often the first sentence (Lesson 19)

transition words words, such as *first*, *next*, or *then*, that help readers connect ideas (Lesson 19)

vary sentence structure to use different sentence types and lengths in your writing (Lesson 26)

Venn diagram a graphic organizer of three overlapping circles that shows how two people or things are alike and how they are different (Lesson 18)

verb a word that shows action or a state of being (Lessons 24–26)

verb tense the form of a verb that shows when an action happens (Lesson 25)

vowel the letters *a, e, i, o,* and *u* in the English language (Lesson 1)

web a graphic organizer that has the topic or main idea in the center oval and supporting ideas or details in ovals around it (Lesson 19)

Mechanics Toolbox

 ## Subject-Verb Agreement

The **subject** tells who or what a sentence is about. The **verb** tells what the subject does. Some subjects are singular. Other subjects are plural.

Examples:

The <u>sun</u> shines.

The <u>dogs</u> bark.

The sun is a singular subject. There is just one sun. *The dogs* is a plural subject. There is more than one dog. The verbs *shines* and *bark* tell what each subject does.

A subject and verb need to match in number, or **agree**.

Examples:

<u>Franklin runs</u> up the hill. (correct)

The <u>little boy run</u> to catch up with his big sister. (incorrect)

The plural verb, *run*, does not agree with the singular subject, *The little boy*. The correct sentence is:

The little boy runs to catch up with his big sister.

 ## Pronoun-Antecedent Agreement

A **pronoun** is a word that takes the place of a noun. An **antecedent** is the word that a pronoun replaces.

Example:

The ducklings followed their mother in a line along the shore. Then they plopped into the lake after her.

In the second sentence, the words *they* and *her* are pronouns. The antecedent of *they* is the plural noun *ducklings*. The antecedent of *her* is the singular noun *mother*.

Pronouns and antecedents need to agree. If the antecedent is more than one, the pronoun needs to show more than one. If the antecedent is male, female, or neither, the pronoun also needs to be male, female, or neither.

Examples:

<u>Geoff</u> read another chapter of the mystery before <u>he</u> went to bed. (correct)

<u>Jessica and Stacey</u> walked to the park. <u>She</u> had a picnic there. (incorrect)

The singular pronoun, *She,* does not agree with the antecedent. *Jessica and Stacey* is more than one. It needs a plural pronoun. The correct sentence is:

Jessica and Stacey walked to the park. They had a picnic there.

 ## Words for Effect

Good writing uses vivid words. Compare these examples:

The girls <u>went happily</u> across the lawn. (weak word choices)

The girls <u>skipped</u> and <u>giggled</u> across the lawn. (strong word choices)

The words *skipped* and *giggled* are strong and vivid. They help the reader "see" the girls.

Using more words is not always better. Vivid words can say a lot on their own. Compare these examples:

The crowd <u>made a lot of noise</u>. (weak word choices)

The crowd <u>roared</u>. (strong word choice)

 ## Adjectives and Adverbs

An **adjective** tells more about a noun. The underlined words in these sentences are adjectives.

Jasmine's bicycle is <u>blue</u>.

Artie ate his <u>favorite</u> meal of spaghetti and meatballs.

The adjective *blue* tells more about the noun *bicycle*. It tells about the color of the bicycle. The adjective *favorite* tells more about the noun *meal*. It tells that the meal is the one Artie likes best.

An **adverb** tells more about a verb, adjective, or another adverb. It answers the question *How?* The underlined words in these sentences are adverbs.

The cat slinked <u>quietly</u> out of the room.

We were happy to go swimming on that <u>very</u> hot Saturday.

The adverb *quietly* tells how the cat slinked. The adverb *very* tells how hot that Saturday was.

Complete Sentences

A sentence tells a complete thought. It has a subject and a verb.

Example:

We laughed.

This sentence is short, but it is complete. It has a subject, *We*. The verb, *laughed*, tells what the subject does.

Some sentences tell two or more complete thoughts. Words like *and*, *but*, and *or* are used to connect the thoughts. In the following sentence, the complete thoughts are underlined.

Dark clouds covered the sky, and rain began to fall.

In other sentences, a less important idea is added to a complete thought. Words like *when*, *because*, *if*, and *after* are used to connect the less important idea to the main thought. In the following sentences, the less important idea is underlined once and the main thought is underlined twice.

My father wakes up when the birds begin to sing.

Because he leaves for work so early, my father also comes home early.

A **run-on sentence** tells two or more thoughts without using any connecting words.

Example:

The sirens grew louder and louder, the fire trucks rushed down the avenue.

You can correct a run-on sentence by splitting it into two complete sentences. You can also correct it by adding a connecting word.

Examples:

The sirens grew louder and louder. The fire trucks rushed down the avenue.

The sirens grew louder and louder, and the fire trucks rushed down the avenue.

A **sentence fragment** does not tell a complete thought.

Example:

The panda that was just born at the zoo.

The subject, *The panda*, does not have a verb. You can correct a sentence fragment by completing the thought. The fragment is completed by adding a verb.

Example:

The panda that was just born at the zoo is still too young for visitors to see.

Confused Words

Homophones are two or more words that sound alike but are spelled differently and mean different things. They are easy to confuse. Here are some homophones.

Homophones and Meanings	Examples
A lot: many **Allot:** to give out	Janice used <u>a lot</u> of fruit to make a big salad for the party. We will <u>allot</u> five cards to each player.
Board: a plank **Bored:** uninterested, dull	We need just one more <u>board</u> to complete our tree house. On the second day of the car trip, Terrence was <u>bored</u>.
Hear: to take in sounds **Here:** at this place	We could <u>hear</u> the children shouting before we saw them. We keep a spare key <u>here</u>, under this rock.
It's: it is **Its:** belonging to it	<u>It's</u> not likely to snow in June. The garden is famous for <u>its</u> prize-winning roses.
Knew: past tense of *know* **New:** opposite of *old*	Johnny <u>knew</u> the name of every student at his school. Angela wore her <u>new</u> bracelet the day after her birthday.
Their: belonging to them **There:** at that place **They're:** they are	<u>Their</u> house has a big porch, whereas ours has none. If you go <u>there</u> to visit, they will ask you to stay for lunch. <u>They're</u> friendly and enjoy company.
Weak: Opposite of *strong* **Week:** A series of seven days	The baby birds were still too <u>weak</u> to fly. In one more <u>week</u> our vacation will begin.

Other words are also commonly confused. Some of them are nearly homophones. Some of them are similar in both sound and meaning. Here are some examples.

Commonly Confused Words and Meanings	Examples
Accept: to agree **Except:** not including	I hope that you <u>accept</u> our invitation to play in the recital! Everyone had fun at the game <u>except</u> for Russell, who was too tired.
Affect: to cause a change **Effect:** result	I cried, but the end of the movie did not <u>affect</u> my mother. The floods were not the only <u>effect</u> of the heavy rains.
Close: to shut **Clothes:** garments, such as a shirt or pants	Mrs. Lee asked me to <u>close</u> the door behind me. I wore my best <u>clothes</u> to the wedding, including the red tie my grandfather gave me.
Loose: opposite of *tight* **Lose:** opposite of *win*	My shoelaces were <u>loose</u>, and I almost tripped on them. It never feels good to <u>lose</u>.
Than: in comparison with **Then:** at that time	My sister likes playing soccer much more <u>than</u> I do. We did not know as much <u>then</u> as we do now.
Weather: the state of the atmosphere in a place **Whether:** shows a choice	The <u>weather</u> here changes quickly, from sunshine to snow in moments. <u>Whether</u> or not you come with me, I am going swimming.

The verbs *lie* and *lay* are also commonly confused. Their meanings are similar. Also, the past tense of *lie* is *lay*. However, *lie* never has an object. *Lay* always has an object. Here are some examples.

Lie: to rest, recline **Lay:** past tense of *lie*	Go <u>lie</u> on the bed until you feel better. Thomas <u>lay</u> there until dinner was ready.
Lay: to put down **Laid:** past tense of *lay*	I <u>lay</u> the flowers on the table. Irma <u>laid</u> the tools she needed on the counter.

 ## Word Choice

Good writing uses exact words. Compare these examples:

The boy was <u>tired</u>.

The boy was <u>sleepy</u>.

The boy was <u>worn out</u>.

Sleepy and *tired* have similar meanings. The word *sleepy* gives more information than the word *tired*. It tells the way the boy is tired: he needs sleep. The word *sleepy* is a more exact word than *tired*.

Worn out and *tired* also have similar meanings. *Worn out* is also more exact than *tired*. It tells that the boy is tired from playing or working hard.

Like vivid words, exact words can say a lot on their own. Compare these examples:

The class <u>had a good time</u> at the farm. (weak word choice)

The class <u>enjoyed</u> the farm. (strong word choice)

Here are some weak words and some stronger words you can use in their place.

Weak Words	Strong Words
Cold	• chilly • frozen • wintery
Warm	• boiling • burning • tropical
Big	• huge • giant • vast
Small	• puny • slight • tiny
Happy	• delighted • pleased • thrilled
Sad	• depressed • gloomy • miserable

Punctuation

Every sentence ends with a punctuation mark. A sentence that tells a statement ends with a **period (.)**. For example:

> We go to the farmers' market on Saturday mornings.

A sentence that gives a command also ends with a period. For example:

> Please get me a pound of apples when you are there.

A sentence that asks a question ends with a **question mark (?)**. For example:

> Does anyone sell fresh eggs at the market?

A sentence that shows excitement ends with an **exclamation point (!)**. For example:

> That pumpkin weighs 300 pounds!

A **quotation** shows the exact words that someone said. A quotation begins and ends with **quotation marks (" ")**. For example:

> Rami said, "Those cider doughnuts are the best."

Notice that a **comma (,)** is used before the quotation. In the following example, a comma is used at the end of the quotation.

> "I like the doughnuts from our bakery better," Allison said.

If the quotation asks a question, a question mark is used. If the quotation shows excitement, an exclamation point is used.

> Examples:

> "Is the market also open on Wednesdays?" Rami asked.

> "I wish it were open every day!" Allison exclaimed.

Notes

Notes

Notes

Notes

Notes